DEATH, DISEASE, DISASTER, & DESPICABLE EVIL

DEATH, DISEASE, DISASTER, & DESPICABLE EVIL

FINDING PEACE IN THE FACE OF TRAGEDY

DR. MICHAEL MESSINA

PALMETTO
P U B L I S H I N G
Charleston, SC
www.PalmettoPublishing.com

For more information, email info@drmessina.com

Hardcover ISBN: 9798822963566
Paperback ISBN: 9798822963573
eBook ISBN: 9798822963580

Acknowledgments

I would like to thank my wife, Tawny, and our two sons, Christopher and Joshua, for their continual encouragement, patience, and sacrifice throughout this project. Thank you for always believing this was possible.

I would like to thank my mom, whose strength has been a source of inspiration through her own tragedies. Thank you for never giving up.

I would like to thank my friends, all those who read the preliminary draft of this book, and those who have endorsed it. Thank you for your honest feedback and support.

I would like to thank my practice office manager, Nancy Salazar, for her devotion to our mission to help people and for her exceptional management of the practice.

I would like to thank my editor, Amy Morgan, for her countless hours, thoroughness, and expertise to help produce the work you are now reading.

I would like to thank the team from Palmetto Publishing for the cover design, formatting, and distribution of this book.

Last and most importantly, I would like to thank God, who has brought me through many tragedies and has shown me his amazing grace and love through them all.

Dedication

This book is dedicated to my wife and sons.
You have been my inspiration.
I love you immeasurably.

Staying Connected

Dr. Michael Messina is a practicing psychologist with a group practice in Southlake, Texas.

Check us out at www.drmessina.com

We regularly post articles on our website related to mental health and well-being.

If you'd like to subscribe to our blog posts and receive news on upcoming books, please sign up on our website above.

Or reach out directly at info@drmessina.com

Also, be sure to Like and Follow Us on our social media!

https://www.facebook.com/drmessinacounseling/

https://www.instagram.com/drmessinaandassociates/

**Thank you for your support.
We look forward to connecting with you!**

Contents

Introduction

Allison, a young mom of three in her thirties, was just diagnosed with stage four breast cancer. Matthew, a single dad of a seven-year-old girl, just found out his daughter was molested by a daycare provider. Lisa's husband of twenty-three years just announced that he is leaving her for another woman. David and Paula are mourning the loss of their son in a fatal drunk-driving accident. Andrew and Sonia are trying to rebuild their lives after a flood destroyed their home. Tyler and Rachel have an infant son with Down Syndrome and profound intellectual disabilities. Brittany was just held at gunpoint during a home invasion.

Death, disease, disaster, and despicable evil. Allow me to introduce you to the world we live in. It's a world of tragedy and suffering that I, as a clinical psychologist, wasn't entirely prepared to face. At age twenty-seven, I had experienced little tragedy in comparison to what I encountered in the therapy room. My first client was a ten-year-old boy at a domestic violence shelter for abused women and their children. The last man he saw before me beat up his mom in front of him. The boy was drawing pictures of people with their heads severed from their bodies, rolling down a hill into a lake. I asked him who the headless people were, and he said, "My family." As a newly married young man with other career options, I thought, "What did I get myself into?"

The journey of practicing as a clinical psychologist has been exhilarating. I've done thousands of hours of psychotherapy and have heard stories of tragedy that would freeze the blood in your veins. People don't typically see a psychologist unless they are suffering. Tragedies like rape, incest, abuse—physical, sexual, and emotional—robbery, homicide, suicide, miscarriages, fatal or disabling accidents, chronic pain, self-harm, and addiction have filled my office for nearly the last two decades. And not to mention the sad realities of hallucinations, delusions, deformities, disabilities, chronic disease, and mental incapacities that people were born with or developed later in life. These are the tragic, day-to-day realities that are affecting millions of people worldwide and in your community, and maybe even you.

But you don't have to be a psychologist to hear stories like this. Turn on any news channel or social media platform. You may find more larger-scale stories, rather than individual ones, but behind every macro event is a person. A person who, like my clients, is left to pick up the rubble that is left of their life after a tragedy. War, genocide, terrorism, mass shootings, sex trafficking, starvation, fatal infectious diseases, tsunamis, fires, and political unrest are in just some of the recent headlines. We are bombarded with tragedy every day. Many of you have experienced these types of tragedies personally or know of someone who has. How do we make sense of a world that seems to be filled with so much pain and suffering?

Many cases are much less severe than these extreme examples. And you may be reading this introduction thinking, "*I have never been through something as horrible as this*," or "*I'm suffering, but it's not due to some massive tragedy like you're describing*." Suffering is very personal. What you are suffering is difficult for you, though it may not affect someone else as much. And regardless of the varying degrees of difficulty people have over the tragedy they are experiencing, for the individual going through it, it's extremely challenging. You, reading this book, are going through something that is hard for you, and that is what is important. *Tragedy* is defined by Merriam-Webster as a "disastrous event." Based on this definition, tragedy is very personal. If it is disastrous for you, then it's a tragedy.

This book is not just for people who have experienced major tragedies, like losing a child to cancer or being paralyzed from a car accident. It's for people with normal, everyday difficulties like job layoffs, midlife crises, infertility, housing and stock market crashes, being parents of a rebellious teen, marital difficulty, nonfatal injuries and illnesses, and problems that are caused by the deceit, selfishness, pride, and hatred of others. "Minor" tragedies are no less painful, and are potentially as harmful, as the others described. Maybe less likely to become a headline, but no less difficult, and just as complex.

This book is for people who have experienced a tragedy of any type and are experiencing painful emotions resulting from it. It is not unusual, following a tragedy, to feel distressing emotions such as anxiety, depression, or anger, and sometimes two or all of these at once. These emotions can range from mild to severe and can be debilitating. If you have experienced tragedy in your life, it is likely that you are experiencing one or more of these emotions.

Where Painful Emotions Come From

Painful emotions like anxiety, depression, and anger are normal reactions following tragedy. If any of the tragedies described so far occurred in your life, you would likely feel a measure of one or more of these emotions. They are the same emotions that most commonly present in a psychotherapy room. These are the emotions people want help with. Most people don't like feeling anxious, depressed, or angry, even when those feelings are justified, and they want relief.

First, it's important to recognize that the feelings (or emotions) I am describing can be experienced by anyone, whether they have been through a tragedy or not, and not everyone who experiences a tragedy has them. Second, these emotions range on a spectrum from mild to severe and can improve or worsen throughout a person's life. They are not static; they ebb and flow, sometimes several times in a day. Third, having anxiety, depression, or anger does not mean that you have a mental disorder. A mental disorder is a strictly defined set of symptoms in the *Diagnostic and Statistical Manual of Mental Disorders, Fifth Edition, Text Revision (DSM-5-TR)*.[1] This is the current manual used by mental health professionals to diagnose mental and emotional disorders. If you are experiencing painful emotions in response to a tragedy, you *may* have an emotional disorder described in this manual, or you may not. Either way, you are experiencing an emotional response that is uncomfortable to you. Understanding a bit more about it will give you the ability to overcome it.

A brief note on this before we move on. My field, the field of psychology, has gravely over-medicalized emotions by labeling normal responses to tragedy as disorders. Doing this creates the potential for communicating that there is something wrong with what you are feeling, and even something wrong with you. A mother who has lost her child to cancer should not be told she has a disorder. No, she needs space to grieve and even be depressed. Suffering over the loss of a child is not wrong or strange. It would be strange *not* to suffer in this circumstance. Our modern Western society has lost all sense of the acceptance of suffering, even emotional suffering, as a normal part of life, so we try to label it and alleviate it as soon as possible. My approach in this book is to leave appropriate space to *feel* when you have experienced a tragedy, because feeling painful emotions is not harmful or wrong.

My intention is to not get caught up in the weeds on whether you have or do not have what meets the medical criteria for an emotional disorder (e.g., an anxiety disorder). That would be unhelpful to you, at least coming from this book. My approach is to take anxiety, depression, and anger as they are, and without medicalizing them, treat them as emotional responses to tragedy that you wish to manage or overcome as you process your tragedy. Yes, you want to grieve, and you should. But you also want to feel better, and you don't want your tragedy or your emotions to consume you.

We need help understanding these emotions and where they come from. We don't go straight from experiencing a tragedy to feeling anxious, depressed, or angry. There's something in between. The in between is our thoughts. *How* we think and *what* we think about lead to our emotions. When people come to psychotherapy because they want to feel better, I don't go straight into trying to fix their problem. Many problems can't be fixed, and I may not be qualified to do so anyway. Feeling better starts with learning to think differently, possibly thinking differently about your emotions and thinking differently about your tragedy. I will not suggest that how you think is wrong or bad and needs to be fixed, as if your thoughts are broken. No feelings are inherently wrong or bad and need to be fixed. Anxiety, depression, and anger may be the appropriate response to a situation. And how you think may be valid.

I do suggest that people often experience relief from their emotional difficulties when they start to see things from a different angle, an alternate perspective they may not have previously considered. This change comes when the therapist points out an alternative way of seeing the problem, or even better, when the person who is suffering begins seeing their problem in a different way through discussion ("getting it all out") and reflective thinking prompted by thoughtful questions. This change of mind is often what helps people get unstuck from emotions they have been struggling with. We'll revisit this topic later in this introduction. For now, let's turn to considering how we have come to view suffering in our modern Western society, and how that view may affect us.

Rethink Suffering

Imagine living in America in the 1800s. You and your spouse have five children and know you will bury at least two of them before their fifth birthday. The remaining three children, like you and your spouse, will live until their midforties, provided no one contracts smallpox, cholera, typhus, dysentery, yellow fever, scarlet fever, measles, malaria, or diphtheria. Then the chances of survival are minimal, and depending on your illness, you and your family will live the rest of your days or weeks with pain, fever, diarrhea, vomiting, yellow skin, blisters, rashes, seizures, blindness, delirium, or paralysis.

If you were "lucky" and wealthy, you may have been able to see a doctor, who may have treated you with mercury, causing your teeth to fall out, gangrene to develop in your mouth, and possibly death. Or you could have been prescribed arsenic, leading to organ failure and death. For rashes or blisters, a hot iron may have been applied to your skin. For certain conditions that were believed to be caused by the patient's blood, veins may have been opened in your limbs and leeches applied to suck the illness out. To stop the spread of gangrene to the rest of your body from a serious wound, limbs may have been amputated with a bone saw, and before 1846, there was no anesthesia.

Broken limbs were often left untreated. Babies born with blindness, deformities, or intellectual disabilities were often killed at birth or institutionalized. Patients who were considered "mentally ill" were often locked into insane asylums or put in cages, and in the late 1800s, several were lobotomized.

The differences in mortality expectancy, wound and disease prognosis, and medical treatments 200 years ago are just one example of the chasm between life then and now. I don't like camping. One, because I'm not good at it, and two, I just don't really like making a shelter and going without controlled temperature for one night. And this is a complaint from someone with a popup tent, precut logs, and a lighter. Two hundred years ago, everyone "camped." And they did it without any of the things that I bring camping. I tell my wife that when the zombie apocalypse happens, we're going to die. Not because of the zombies, but because her husband doesn't know how to grow or kill food. She says, "You'd figure it out." I'm not so sure.

As I sit in my comfortable chair in my office, typing on my laptop, with wireless internet, with my cell phone next to me, in perfectly controlled temperature, drinking coffee made in a Keurig, and several options for breakfast in the next room, I am shaking my head over what I now find "necessary" and can't live without, forgetting that until relatively recently none of this existed. As I think about all that my children have, compared to what our grandparents, and especially our great-grandparents, had when they were children, three things are clear. First, we have it easy. Second, we have forgotten how to suffer. And third, we are totally unprepared emotionally for when a real tragedy does strike us.

Advancements in technology and medicine in the twenty-first century have eliminated much of our suffering. Don't get me wrong. I'm glad that smallpox has been eradicated. I'm glad that I was able to get sinus surgery and I don't remember a thing from it. I like driving in my car with heated leather seats in the winter. I like going to the grocery store and being able to choose from fifty different coffee flavors. But all these comforts have made us *soft*. We, as a people, as a society, used to be a lot tougher. Our ancestors would probably shake their heads in disbelief about some of the things we complain about and find hard.

But who could blame us? We strive as a society to eliminate all forms of suffering: physical, social, legal, environmental, financial, and psychological. And we have all forms of professionals to help us do that. Medical researchers advance the field of medicine to remove as much suffering as possible through the development of new drugs and surgical procedures. Dietitians and fitness trainers also help us "live well." Sociologists, social workers, lawyers, environmentalists, and lawmakers all strive to raise awareness, enact policy, and create systemic changes to right wrongs, eliminate injustice, and provide opportunities for advancement. And of course, money can buy lots of comforts and can in many ways ease suffering. Psychologists and mental health professionals are trained to help people manage emotional suffering.

The quest to ease suffering is not in opposition to biblical teaching, by the way. There are passages that support the practice of creating a society focused on advancing the common good and repressing wrongdoing and injustice—in short, the fight to end suffering. And there's nothing wrong with enjoying certain comforts that God provides. There's no glory in allowing suffering to continue when we have the means to stop it. So, what is the problem with creating a comfortable culture like ours to counter the grim realities of tragedy and suffering?

We have convinced ourselves that happiness and comfort are the main goals of life. But even the word *goal* falls short of what we mean. *Purpose* is more like it. We have convinced ourselves that the purpose of life is to be happy and comfortable. We have turned the pursuit of happiness, that inalienable right that our founding fathers saw, into a purpose that drives all of life. It's not just a right anymore, it's a life aim. Our society supports this belief, and the church has not been successful in turning our minds from it. *Health, wealth,* and *happiness,* if not said explicitly from the pulpit, are woven into our Christian sermons, books, and programs. Selfism, the newest "Christian" religion, has crept its way into our sanctuaries, promoting a self-improvement gospel message. As C. S. Lewis said, "We want, in fact, not so much a Father in heaven as a grandfather in heaven—a senile benevolence who, as they say, 'liked to see young people enjoying themselves' and whose plan for the universe was simply that it might be truly said at the end of each day, 'a good time was had by all.'"[2]

As Timothy Keller rightly pointed out in his book, *Walking with God through Pain and Suffering,*[3] we have removed all purpose and meaning from suffering, and have made it unacceptable and antithetical to our purpose of happiness and comfort. If you are suffering, something is wrong, and the suffering or the thing causing the suffering needs to be stomped out immediately. There is no place for suffering *well* or finding purpose or meaning in your suffering. There is no place for it in society, in church, or in God. Tragedy and suffering are considered "in the way" of life's aim. We completely miss the search for any meaning that tragedy and suffering might bring to our lives. Suffering, in a society such as we have created, can have no meaning or object. It's simply a barrier to happiness, our ultimate purpose.

Because we are so accustomed to comfort, so unaccustomed to suffering, and so convinced that all forms of suffering are a barrier to our ultimate aim of happiness, we crumble to pieces mentally and emotionally when tragedy strikes. We simply can't handle it. We have no place in our minds to allow for tragedy. Life is supposed to be comfortable. We believe that everything that happens in life should support our belief in a perfectly comfortable existence. How could I pursue happiness when this tragedy is in the way? But it really is in the way. And when all has been done to try to fix the problem, and we are left with a situation that is unfixable, we are forced either to completely collapse into misery and despair that life has dealt us such a hand, or to change our paradigm entirely. If you have already experienced tragedy in your life, this book will help you think in a way that will help you through it. If you have not already experienced tragedy, this book will help you prepare emotionally for that eventuality.

Rethink God

Most of society lives as though God does not exist, even if they believe in him. And if they do believe he exists, they believe in a passive God, uninvolved in the day-to-day affairs on this earth. God is optional. "If it works for you, that's great. I'm happy you've found religion. But don't put your regulations on me," is the common way of thinking. We live in a postmodern world, where there are no objective standards or truths by which to live (never mind that claiming there are no objective standards is itself a claim of an objective standard). Most people live without the concept of a God who knows every thought of their mind, inclination of their heart, and action in the dark. A God who cares, died on a cross, and will one day return to judge the world.

Who do we really believe is regulating the activities on this earth? Humankind, Satan, or chance? Christians say that God is in control all the time, but do we really believe it? And what do we mean by it exactly? When we read some of the "all things" scriptures, like God "works *all things* according to the counsel of his will" (Ephesians 1:11, emphasis mine), "*All things* were created through him and for him" (Colossians 1:16, emphasis mine), and "From him and through him and to him are *all things*" (Romans 11:36, emphasis mine), do we think that the "all things" means everything except tragedy? Have we removed all calamity, tragedy, and suffering from what is included in "all things"? *All things* means all things. *All* things (including tragedy) are worked according to the counsel of his will and are from him, through him, for him, and to him.

I think Christians today are trying to wrap our heads around this reality, but we have been taught that God is up there, not down here, regulating the affairs of this world. Sure, he's in control of the tsunamis and hurricanes, but how about the individual decisions of politicians or the terrorist cells in the US plotting the next 9/11? Does God govern the stars in the sky, but not the events that affect the people he made in his own image?

We fall to pieces when tragedy strikes, not only because we have forgotten how to suffer and because we have set as our target the wrong purposes in life, but also because we don't know the God of the Bible. But this is not totally our fault. We, as a church society, have backslid from the rock-solid biblical teachings about the sovereignty of God over and through all, and have settled for an impotent Christianity, one that says God wants peace on earth but can't control the whims of humans or Satan, and therefore, "anything goes." Sure, we believe that God works all things together for good (Romans 8:28), but he works after the fact, and never creates or plans tragedy for his people.

We need to remember that it was God who said, "I form light and create darkness; I make well-being and create calamity; I am the Lord, who does all these things" (Isaiah 45:7). And the words of Jeremiah, "Who has spoken and it came to pass, unless the Lord has commanded it? Is it not from the mouth of the Most High that good and bad come?" (Lamentations 3:37–38). And the words of Job, who said, "Shall we receive good from God, and shall we not receive evil?" (Job 2:10). And the words of Amos, "Does disaster come to a city, unless the Lord has done it?" (Amos 3:6). These scriptures are a droplet of water in a sea of scriptures regarding God's rule over this earth, good, and evil.

And let's be careful not to play divine referee on God's playing field. We are quick to judge what we think is good or bad, right or wrong, virtuous or evil. As we move through this book, let's remember Isaiah 55:8–9, which says:

> "For my thoughts are not your thoughts,
>   neither are your ways my ways, declares the LORD.
> For as the heavens are higher than the earth,
>   so are my ways higher than your ways
>   and my thoughts than your thoughts."

God's ways do not always align with our opinion on how things should go. Isaiah 40:13–14 says:

> Who has measured the Spirit of the LORD,
>   or what man shows him his counsel?
> Whom did he consult,
>   and who made him understand?
> Who taught him the path of justice,
>   and taught him knowledge,
>   and showed him the way of understanding?

God does not consult us when he does something. He doesn't ask our opinion. He consults only the counsel of his own will (Ephesians 1:11), which is "good and acceptable and perfect" (Romans 12:2).

Scope of Influence
It was nearly twenty years ago that I stepped into the practice of psychotherapy, and a lot of *life* has happened since then. My introduction to

dealing with personal tragedy had begun several years earlier, as I was forced to cope with the aftermath of my dad's depression and his eventual suicide, which I'll share more about in Chapter 1. Several other events have occurred that have caused me to think hard about life and God.

I had a pretty wild upbringing, and it's a miracle I didn't die before my twentieth birthday, when I became a Christian. Fights happened every weekend in my childhood neighborhood, and there was a constant fear of getting jumped or shot by rival peers that didn't like my friend group. I got beat up pretty bad in two of the fights I was in. We were drunk or high almost all the time. Guys and girls cheated on each other constantly, and you couldn't trust friends or girlfriends. The men around me were not great influences: infidelity, divorce, drugs, alcohol, and violence were some of the behaviors my friends and I witnessed. Of my friend group in high school, one is serving a lifetime sentence for murder, at least four were drug addicts, one was killed in a knife fight, and two died in a drunk-driving accident when their car veered off the road.

Since my dad's passing and the death of my friends in a car accident, I have experienced much more death. A friend of my wife and me, a young mom with two kids, died of breast cancer a few years after that. My senior pastor, who married my wife and me, died at fifty-nine of a heart attack. My wife's close friend in college died of cancer in her forties. My clinical supervisor died. My psychologist friend died from stomach cancer. My wife's dad died from diabetes complications. My three remaining living grandparents died. Four friends from church, around my age, died: one from cancer, one from sickle cell anemia, one from dehydration after getting lost hiking in Death Valley, and one shot himself in the head with his pistol.

Illness, as well, has not spared us, though God's mercy in these illnesses has sustained us. In 2009 I was diagnosed with a neurological autoimmune disease called multiple sclerosis (MS), which I will discuss in Chapter 2. In 2016 my wife started having grand mal seizures in her sleep. After three years, multiple tests, and many more seizures, she was diagnosed with adult-onset epilepsy. These are just the big things. There are countless other, smaller things that have challenged our faith over the years, covering the difficulties of child rearing, moving across states, housing and financial losses, and psychological pain.

These tragedies, combined with all the tragedies I have observed through my clients' lives, have caused me to think deeply about the subject of tragedy and suffering. I have experienced and seen firsthand the emotional impact tragedy can have, and I believe we can experience relief by *thinking differently*. However, I have not experienced every tragedy that you have experienced. And the tragedies I have experienced may be a walk in Disneyland compared to what you have suffered through. There are many tragedies that I have, at least at this point in my life, been spared. I have learned as a psychologist, and as a pastor prior to that, that I can't possibly relate to every single tragedy that people go through, and I feel the constant tension of trying to help people through things I have not experienced. I may not know what it is like to walk in your shoes, but I know my own shoes hurt. I hope that the words in this book can minister to both of us so we can walk with a little less pain.

I am not a trained theologian, a historian, or an expert in biblical languages. While I did serve as a pastor for two years, my career has been primarily in the field of mental health as a psychologist. So I am writing as a psychologist who has a deep commitment to the Christian faith, the authority of Scripture, and the supremacy of Jesus Christ. My aim is to relate and discuss, through the lens of these commitments, the suffering that I have experienced through my clients, undergone in my own life, and seen in the world. My goal is that this lens will provide a suitable vantage point from which to see the problem of pain and suffering in a way that provides healing. This is not a book on theology, though we will touch on theological points at various times and in various ways, as good theology is necessary to see the world accurately and is therapeutic. This is a self-help book for Christians who are suffering. Nothing more. And by *therapeutic*, I don't mean that good theology is optional, or that the main goal of theology is personal growth. However, our theology, that is, what we believe about God, will affect how we think, and how we think does affect how we feel.

Nothing that I say in this book about God and his actions and involvement in this world with relation to tragedy and suffering originated with me. I did not receive some special revelation or find something new that hasn't been discovered before. I do not have some special corner on the truth, my word is not the end of the matter, and I don't claim to have all of this figured out. We are dealing with the greatest problem in all of history: the problem of suffering in the world. This has been discussed and debated for centuries and will no doubt continue to be discussed until Jesus returns. There are things we simply don't know, and we will have to be settled with not knowing, because in God's infinite wisdom, he has not revealed everything to us.

Several authors and thinkers have helped me along my journey to a deeper understanding of this problem of suffering in the world. Many of the thoughts in this book have already been written by Aurthur W. Pink, Charles H. Spurgeon, C. S. Lewis, Elisabeth Elliot, Jerry Bridges, John Calvin, John Flavel, Jonathan Edwards, Joni Eareckson Tada, John Piper, Martin Luther, Paul Helm, R. C. Sproul, Stephen Charnock, and Timothy Keller. For a deeper study on the problem of suffering in the world, a list of resources has been compiled at the end of this book.

The wisdom of these men and women has ministered profoundly to me in my hours of desperate need for answers, and they have greatly influenced my way of thinking about God in relation to tragedy. But I want to be clear that I assume full responsibility for any errors contained in this book. I own them. And everything right is a product of what I have learned, studied, and been shown by others and by God in his word and through the Holy Spirit in my pursuit of the truth. I have done my painstaking best to present the word of God faithfully and accurately in regard to the subject matter at hand. I want to encourage you to read this book with an open heart, study the scriptures and material presented, and see what you think for yourself. As the Apostle Paul said, "Test everything; hold fast what is good" (1 Thessalonians 5:21).

Outline

This book, *Death, Disease, Disaster & Despicable Evil: Finding Peace in the Face of Tragedy*, was written to help Christians experience emotional healing from painful emotions during and following tragedy. I believe that by thinking differently about many of the conceptions we hold about God, tragedy, our own lives, and the world around us, we can experience true peace and joy even in the severest trials. Anxiety, depression, and anger are the most common emotions expressed by people who have gone through tragedy. These emotions can be debilitating, but they don't have to be. By learning to think differently, we can manage and overcome them. God, through his word, has shown us a way to think about suffering that will lead to emotional healing.

Each of the four sections of this book presents a decidedly biblical, Christian worldview on tragedy and suffering.

- Section I, "Finding Peace in Our Thoughts," covers our thought patterns that lead to emotional distress and how to develop new patterns of thinking that will lead to alleviation of emotional symptoms.

- Section II, "Finding Peace in Our Feelings," discusses anxiety, depression, and anger, and a biblical understanding of each.

- Section III, "Finding Peace in Our Tragedies," covers ways to think about the four major tragedies covered in this book.

  - "Death" covers all types of death throughout the lifespan.

  - "Disease" includes a discussion on diseases, illnesses, accidents, and disabilities.

  - "Disaster" covers natural disaster and those caused by human error or negligence.

  - "Despicable Evil" covers those tragedies caused by the sinful actions and intentions of people.

- Section IV, "Finding Peace in Our Suffering," presents a framework by which we can understand the suffering in this world that is caused by tragedy and learn to find peace in it.

Journal Questions

My aim is to help you think differently about God, your tragedy, and the world of suffering around us, so that you can feel better during your current tragedy and be better prepared for future ones. My method is to provide a thorough and thoughtful discussion on this subject throughout this book, in order to guide our thoughts and help our feelings. As in my therapy practice, change happens through a dynamic process of thought-provoking questions and dialogue. I have included at the end of each chapter a list of reflective journal questions that are meant to be thought about and answered through journaling.

Journaling is a way of processing our thoughts and emotions. It's a way of thinking (by writing) that allows us to really think through our thoughts (*metacognition*), process what is going on, connect with our thoughts and emotions, and come to realizations and commitments. It's a way to work things out, or figure things out, and is a type of therapy with your thoughts, an exercise that is very helpful and highly recommended. The process of journaling through the questions at the end of each chapter will help you synthesize and internalize what you have learned, make each concept practical, and move toward inner healing. In addition, there may be some steps, or behavioral strategies, suggested along with the questions that will help you take what you've learned and put it into practice.

I am biased in favor of paper journaling, that is, journaling with a pen or pencil in a paper notebook of some kind, versus electronic journaling, which is journaling on an electronic device, such as a phone, tablet, or computer. I know this is super old school, but there is something about writing my thoughts on paper that just works for me. The main reason, I think, is because my devices are very distracting. I'll start journaling on my phone, and then before you know it, I'm responding to a text message. But use whatever works for you. There is no right way to journal. It's only important that you are consistent and persistent, because some of the questions are not easily answered, and they are meant to help you process your thoughts and situation. Praying through the questions as you go can also be helpful.

Thank you for taking the time to read this book. The words on these pages, especially the questions and exercises, have helped me through my emotional pain during tragedy, and I believe they will help you as well. Let's begin our journey.

Section I:
Finding Peace in
Our Thoughts

CHAPTER 1

Think Differently

It's amazing what we remember from a day of tragedy. "Where Were You (When the World Stopped Turning)" is the name of the famous country song by Alan Jackson that was released following the terrorist attacks on 9/11. And rightly so. If you were alive in 2001, it's likely that you remember exactly where you were when you got the news. The tragic story I am going to share with you is not the tragedy of 9/11, but a personal tragedy that occurred three months before.

At that time, I was living in Long Beach, California, about twenty minutes from San Pedro, the town I grew up in. I was twenty-three years old, single, and had been living on my own for about two years. I had just received my undergraduate degree and was working as an associate pastor for a local campus ministry at the university I graduated from. It was Saturday, June 9, 2001, around 8:00am. I was at a park in Long Beach just finishing up a morning devotional with a couple of guys from our ministry when I received a page (for those of you who don't know what this is, it's like a text message, but simpler!) from an unfamiliar 310 number, the area code of my hometown.

I found the nearest payphone (yes, it's a phone you put money in to make it work) and called the number. The person said, "Michael, come home!" and hung up. That's it. No name, just "Come home." I knew who it was, and what this call was about. Over the last couple of years, my dad's depression had been intensifying. He had suffered with clinical depression my whole life. As a young child, I thought being depressed was normal. That's just how you are when you get older—not speaking for days, sitting in the same place for hours, almost endless television watching, irritability, and insomnia. These are some of the things I observed. I learned later that I was shielded from knowing about his repeated suicide attempts and hospitalizations throughout my life.

I hung up the phone and started the drive home over the Vincent Thomas Bridge that connects Long Beach to San Pedro, praying and thinking about what I knew I was walking into. When I pulled in to my street, my childhood friend (whom I had just spoken to) flagged me down from his driveway across the street from my house and told me to come inside his house. Upon walking in, the scene was grim and tumultuous. My mom was crying hysterically at the kitchen table, sitting next to her sister, who was also crying hysterically. Her hair was sticking straight up, like she got the news in the middle of doing her hair and drove straight over. I was informed that my dad was dead. He actually did it. He killed himself. I was numb.

Before this, I don't think I had ever seen a dead body. We went over to the house, and there he was, lying on our couch. My dad, dead. I found out that he overdosed on prescription psychiatric medication, the medication that was supposed to help his depression. By this time, my grandparents, my dad's parents, were there. That was heartbreaking. Seeing their son lie dead on the living room couch from suicide was just too much. In the moments, which seemed like hours, that followed, the police came to question my mom to rule out homicide. I was told this was protocol when someone dies in a home. A social worker was there as well, trying to console my grandparents. I'm sure she meant well, but what could she say? Their forty-nine-year-old son lay dead from suicide on a couch in the next room. I had never seen my Sicilian grandfather cry before.

I believe it was the paramedics who asked us to wait outside while they removed the body. What was complete commotion turned into complete silence as they drove away. No one spoke a word. My mom wanted everyone out of her house. I think by this time, neighbors and other relatives were there. The social worker helped get everyone out. Then it was just my mom, my brother, and I, in silence.

The first week after his passing was weird, kind of surreal. I stayed with my mom all week. We tried to do things together. I remember feeling the need to talk about it, so I called my pastor and close friends. Within a few days, a wake was held, followed by the funeral the next day. It was an open-casket wake. My dad lay in his coffin, still and lifeless, wearing a neatly pressed black suit, tie, and white shirt. I've heard people say that their loved ones who have passed look peaceful. He did not look peaceful to me. He didn't *look* anything at all. He, or I should say, his body, was just *there*. I touched his face, and it felt as hard as stone. The funeral was emotionally draining. After the ceremony, my mom, my brother, and I sat in a row in front of his grave while it seemed like hundreds of people walked by, bent down, and hugged and kissed all of us. Many of them were crying and saying how sorry they were for our loss.

At some point, I went back to Long Beach and back to work. My mom and my brother went back to work. Everyone moved on with their lives. Now I have a wife and two teenage boys of my own. My dad would have been seventy-two years old this year, and my kids would have known their grandfather. And I'm getting older. This year I will have lived more time without my dad than with my dad, and in three years, I'll be as old as he was when he died.

I used to ask myself if I ever really processed his death, because I didn't feel a whole lot when he died. I felt numb and shocked for about a week, but after that, things went back to normal. What I didn't know was that my *normal* was the depression, anxiety, and anger I had been suppressing for years. This is how I dealt with emotions; I buried them. So when my dad committed suicide, it didn't really hit me at the time, at least not more than I was already hit. The reality was, I was already living in a steady state of functional depression, anxiety, and anger, and had been my whole life as I watched his depression slowly kill him.

Becoming a Christian at age twenty helped. But that doesn't cure depression, just like becoming a Christian doesn't cure cancer. Initially, I think becoming a Christian provided a supportive Christian community as well as the spiritual tools to cope with depression better, like prayer, Bible study, and meditation. These can all be great practices for dealing with depression and other emotions that arise from experiencing tragedy. But, unless they are used in the process of metacognition described in the introduction, it's like putting a Band-Aid on a wound. It may protect it from getting worse, but what's needed is a healing ointment. Something to get to the root of the problem.

I've learned over the years that what I needed, what my dad needed, and what countless other people going through any tragedy need, is to *think differently*. Our minds, how we think, may be the only thing we can change in a tragedy. As I said in the introduction, some things are unchangeable and unfixable. What can change, though, is how we think about the situation. Prayer, Bible study, meditation, and fellowship with believers are necessary in our Christian walk. And the more these practices help us to think differently about God and our tragic situation, the more relief from our distressing emotions we will experience.

Think Differently, Feel Differently

I did not come up with the idea of changing how we think to change how we feel—not even close. Thinking differently to feel differently is the hallmark of a type of psychotherapy called cognitive behavioral therapy, or CBT for short. CBT is arguably the most widely used and well-established model of psychotherapy available. It's used around the world for a variety of clinical issues, including the emotional challenges addressed in this book, namely anxiety, depression, and anger. CBT was first developed by Aaron Beck[4] in the 1960s and has been written about, studied, and used extensively for the last sixty years. CBT maintains that our feelings and actions are a byproduct of how we think. Specifically, when a situation occurs, how we think, or perceive, the situation will determine how we feel about it and how we act. So, to help someone through their emotional pain, a CBT therapist helps them with their thoughts.

Sarah

Sarah came to see me two years following the death of her mother in an automobile accident. Sarah's mother was driving home early in the morning following her night shift in the hospital, where she worked as a nurse, when a drunk driver slammed into her in a head-on collision. She was killed instantly. The drunk driver took off on foot, but was later caught, arrested, and prosecuted. After two years, Sarah continued to experience intense depression over the loss of her mother, fierce anger toward the driver who killed her, and anger at God, whom Sarah believed let this happen for reasons she could not understand.

After some time, Sarah revealed that she blamed herself for her mom's death. They were supposed to go to dinner and spend time together that night, but Sarah had a big school project due the next day that she had been putting off. She decided to cancel dinner plans with her mom so that she could study and encouraged her mom to take a shift at the hospital instead. Sarah was holding on to her grief as a sort of punishment for herself because of the guilt she was experiencing. Further, Sarah thought her mom would be dishonored in some way if she were to move on with her life. Sarah's anger toward the driver was rooted in her hatred of him because of the selfish and foolish choice he made to drive while intoxicated. Sarah's anger at God went something like, "How could a loving God let such a thing happen? Mom never did anything to hurt anyone. She didn't deserve this. She was young and had so much more to do in her life."

Sarah's healing did not come overnight, and it certainly didn't come by me giving her a different way to think. Sarah's healing came slowly as she learned to think about life and about God in ways that she had never seriously considered before. She had to learn to think differently or remain stuck. I say *learn* because it doesn't come automatically. It's a process. And what does healing look like in a situation like this? Healing from tragedy most often does not mean that you never get depressed, anxious, or angry again when you think about the tragic situation. With severe tragedies, you do not go back to how things were before. A new normal is created. Time, space, and thinking differently do heal emotional wounds, but healing does not mean a complete and permanent reversal of your emotional state.

Sarah will always have a measure of sorrow over her mom's passing. I will always have pain over my dad's suicide. You may always have heartache over your tragic situation. But healing means that we are not paralyzed by it. Healing means that we are not living in a place of depression, anxiety, and anger all the time. Healing means that we do not lose our faith in God over the tragedy, or become bitter and resentful toward him, others, or ourselves. Healing means that we can forgive those who are responsible for the tragedy. It means that we can live from a place of freedom: freedom to feel peace, joy, and gratitude, and freedom to love and serve others with the heart of Christ.

Suffering brings a depth of understanding to the cold, hard realities of this life, this side of heaven. If you've suffered, you will not live a shallow, happy-go-lucky life anymore, if that's how you lived prior to your tragedy. But why should you? And why would you want to? There's too much suffering in the world to spend your life oblivious to it. There's too much pain to ignore it. As John Piper talks about in his book, *Spectacular Sins*,[5] Christians have a strange kind of experience as we live in this world: "sorrowful, yet always rejoicing" (2 Corinthians 6:10). We can have an awareness of what is happening to us and around us, and that does bring sorrow. Real sorrow. But, because of our understanding of God and his care for us in this world, Jesus Christ and his sacrifice for us, our salvation, and the promises given to us, we can simultaneously rejoice.

Sarah struggled with depression and anger for two years after her mother's tragic death. She began to heal when she stopped blaming and punishing herself. The anger toward the man who killed her mother, and God who let it happen, was the hardest emotion to manage. It was true, this man's choice to drive intoxicated killed Sarah's mom. Although he didn't leave the bar saying, "I'm going to try to kill someone on my way home tonight," his actions were irresponsible, reckless, and selfish. The laws of the State rightly hold this man accountable for his choice and the resulting consequences. These things are true, and Sarah has every right to be angry with him for killing her mom. But Sarah's *right* to be angry doesn't make up for the effects that Sarah will experience as a result of carrying around chronic anger for the rest of her life. I mean, if you asked her, she would say she doesn't like feeling this angry all the time. Would you?

And what about God? Couldn't he have stopped it? Could not the God of the universe who commands fire to fall from the sky (1 Kings 18:38), storms to stop (Exodus 9:33), the blind to see (Mark 10:52), and the dead to rise (John 11:44) have stopped this guy from getting into his car that night? Or once in his car, could God have caused his car not to start, or break down before leaving the parking lot? Could God have caused him or Sarah's mom to take a different route or directed traffic in such a way that they wouldn't have crossed paths? Could God have caused Sarah's mom to be sick that night and unable to work? Could God have caused a shortage of alcohol in the bar the man was in, or caused the man to be unable to get to the bar for whatever reason? Maybe he could have had a heart attack or passed out drunk before he drove that night. Or maybe he could have lost his keys. Or maybe the collision could have been at a slightly different angle, which could have resulted in Sarah's mom being injured but not killed.

What do you believe about God? When you believe God is all-powerful, you believe he could do these things. You believe that he who created the world from nothing could do anything and everything. But in the case of Sarah's mom, he did *not* do any of the things we described in the previous paragraph. He could have stopped it but didn't. Why? One *wrong* answer is that he is actually not all-powerful, but that humankind, Satan, and chance have the upper hand. If we rule out that answer, and we will later, then the other wrong answer is that he is not all-loving. Maybe he is all-powerful, but not all-loving: He could have stopped Sarah's mom from dying, but he just doesn't care enough. Most Christians do not believe either of these answers. They believe God is all-powerful *and* all-loving. However, when tragedy strikes, we are all left confused. How do we reconcile a God who is both all-powerful and all-loving in the face of tragedy?

Thinking about Tragedy

Imagine that you and your spouse just got the kids down for bed, and you are sitting on your couch, drinking a glass of wine and watching the next episode of your favorite Netflix series, when six armed men with masks kick open your front door, breaking the deadbolt through the door frame, and storm into your house yelling, "This is the police!" This is what happened to my client, Brittany, and her husband. It was not the police. It was men with guns, and one was now holding one to Brittany's head while dragging her around the house, and they had already beaten and tied up her husband. "Put your cell phones and all your money, jewelry, and guns into this bag or we'll kill you!"

Brittany later tried to recall what was going through her mind at the moment. She had tried to do exactly as they said and kept saying, "Take whatever you want. Please don't hurt us." All they said was, "Shut up!"

She recalled not knowing if these men knew about their children upstairs. She didn't know if they were going to take her children, kill her husband, rape her, or kill her. One of Brittany's daughters came downstairs and saw everything that was happening. One of the men forcefully pushed the little girl to the ground and kept moving. Thankfully, after getting the items they demanded, they left. Only Brittany's husband was physically hurt, and his wounds healed in a few weeks. But the emotional damage to all of them is something that will not heal easily, if at all, if ever.

How do I even begin to help Brittany work through this? As a Christian, Brittany was left with all kinds of questions. Sure, she was thankful that God protected her family during this horrific ordeal, but why didn't God prevent it from happening in the first place? Think about the emotional damage to Brittany's daughter. Following the incident, she regressed to severe separation anxiety and bedwetting, and developed post-traumatic stress disorder (PTSD). Why didn't God stop it? Was he not able to? Doesn't he care? As I said, most Christians are not comfortable with either of these options. What is it, then? If God is all-powerful and all-loving, and tragedy happens all the time, there must be some other answer. We need to think deeper. And for many Christians, we need to think *differently*.

Since most Christians believe that God is all-powerful and all-loving, they are left in this kind of in-between, unclear phase and use clichés like "God is in control." They use partial scriptures like Romans 8:28, "All things work together for good" and 1 Corinthians 10:13 wrongly quoted as, "God will not give you more than you can bear." I am sure that anyone who says these things means well. I've said them before and meant well. But to set the record straight: When you're suffering, these platitudes and partial or incorrect Scripture quotations are *not helpful*! For one, what do they even mean? In Brittany's case, God could have stopped those men from entering. But he didn't. So, him being in control means what, exactly?

And, sure, all things work together for good. I believe that. But in Brittany's case, does this mean that God works after the fact? Like, God didn't want these men to break in, but because they did, God will now show up and work good into it? While I'm grateful that God has the power to now work good into this mess, the fact that it happened at all makes me tremble at the possibility of it happening again. I don't want God to just show up after and make good with it, I want him there the whole time. And, finally, if God only gave us what we can bear, we would never need him. Professional body builders lift weights with a spotter because without one they couldn't make the gains they want. God is our spotter. He gives us *more* than we can handle so that we will rely on him and in the process, get stronger. So let's stop saying that God will only give us what we can bear. I couldn't bear half the things I am bearing now if I didn't first have to bear them with God. For Brittany to move through this nightmare and regain her life, she is going to have to learn to think differently about God, tragedy, and life itself.

God's Method during Tragedy

The Bible is a comprehensive treatise on tragedy and suffering. I say *comprehensive* because from cover to cover, we see the immense struggle of God's people in a variety of contexts and circumstances covering a period of around 4,000 years. In Genesis alone, we see real tragedies of murder, rape, incest, slavery, deceit, and false accusation caused by the hatred, selfishness, lust, and greed of people. Additionally, there's war, severe famine, the destruction of an entire city by a rain of sulfur and fire, and the catastrophic annihilation of the whole world by a flood. Moving to Exodus, God's people are brutally enslaved and mistreated in Egypt for nearly 400 years, leading to their deliverance, which meant widescale suffering for the Egyptians who all woke up to their dead eldest son, and then hundreds or thousands drowned in the Red Sea. The remainder of the Old Testament is filled with betrayal, war, murder (including the murder of children, women, and the elderly), disease, famine, persecution, more slavery, and even the practice of child sacrifice and child cannibalism.

As the New Testament begins, we see God's people under the oppressive rule of the Roman Empire, a brutal reign bent on conquest, overtaxation, control, and cruel punishment for anyone who stepped out of line. It was so bad that certain groups of Jews attempted insurrection through violent means in order to expel Rome from the Holy Land. The Zealots, for example, were trained, underground Jewish assassins constantly plotting the extermination of their foreign occupiers. It was in this setting that our Lord and Savior was born. The suffering and death of Jesus was predicted repeatedly in the Old Testament and was instigated by the Jews and carried out by the Romans with the most brutal execution method in history. Jesus' death and resurrection is then followed by sixty or so years of severe persecution of Christians.

This entire bloody scene is a thread of experience in the Old and New Testaments against the backdrop of a glorious, merciful, compassionate, longsuffering, and all-loving heavenly Father, who is at the same time holy, righteous, and just. Tragedy and suffering in the Bible, just like today, has a variety of causes, such as people's sinful inclinations and choices, the foolish thinking and behavior of people, punishment from God for sinful choices, and discipline, correction, or refinement from God, like what a wise parent uses with their child to shape them into the person the parent knows the child could be.

God and Our Thoughts

When God's people, described in the Bible, experienced various hardships, his method was often to help them think differently—to see or perceive their situation another way. Sometimes this meant God revealing more about himself, as in the case of Job (Job 38–41). Other times it meant God's direct display of his power, as in the case of Elijah (1 Kings 19:11–12). Other times it meant God revealing or reminding of a promise, as in the case of Abraham (Genesis 15:3–5). To reveal more about himself, display his power, or talk about a promise was God's normal way of working when his people were in trouble. And his purpose was to get them to think differently, to see their trouble differently—to see it through the eyes of the one who is greater and stronger than the problem. The Bible is filled with example after example of this. In fact, it might be said that everything God says or does is said or done in order to make us think differently, that is, more in line with how he wants us to think.

God cares about our thoughts.

- The greatest commandment is to love God with all your heart, soul, *mind*, and strength (Mark 12:30).

- Paul told the church in Colosse to bear fruit in every good work and increase "in the knowledge of God" (Colossians 1:10).

- As Christians, we should "take every thought captive to obey Christ" (2 Corinthians 10:5), rather than allowing our thoughts to be led astray (2 Corinthians 11:3).

- With the mind of Christ (1 Corinthians 2:16), our minds should be set on the Spirit (Romans 8:6) and on things above (Colossians 3:2).

- And we should be continually transformed by the renewal of our minds (Romans 12:2).

- And finally, "whatever is true, whatever is honorable, whatever is just, whatever is pure, whatever is lovely, whatever is commendable, if there is any excellence, if there is anything worthy of praise, *think* about these things" (Philippians 4:8, emphasis mine).

It seems that Jesus and the Apostle Paul believed that our thoughts were very important. God, in his infinite wisdom, created this amazing organ inside our head, like a computer, that governs all our thoughts, which leads to decisions, feelings, and actions, all of which God wants centered on him. So, when it comes to helping someone through a tragedy, God works on our thoughts in various ways. Consider the following ten examples:

1. Sarah, while barren, heard God say she would have a son in her old age (Genesis 18:10).

2. Joseph, while in prison, was given favor by the Lord with the prison warden and the ability to interpret dreams (Genesis 39:21, 40:8).

3. Moses, when afraid to talk to Pharoah, was shown miracles (Exodus 4:1–7).

4. Joshua, when told to lead the entire Israelite nation, was told by God that he, God, would be with him (Joshua 1:9).

5. Elijah, while hiding from King Ahab, was brought food by ravens every day (1 Kings 17:6).

6. Elisha and Gehazi, when surrounded by enemy troops, were shown the Lord's invisible army on the mountain, surrounding the enemy troops (2 Kings 6:17).

7. Ezekiel, who had an extremely difficult task, was shown the resurrection of skeletons in the valley of dry bones (Ezekiel 37:7–10).

8. The disciples, when hungry, were given the miracle of food (Luke 9:16–17).

9. When the disciples were afraid of the weather, Jesus stopped the storm (Mark 4:39).

10. When the disciples were afraid of the Roman and Jewish leaders after Jesus' death, he appeared among them (John 20:19).

All of these examples show words or actions by God that are meant to change how people thought in times of tribulation, grief, and fear. In addition to God working to change how they thought in a direct sense within the tribulation, grief, and fear that was going on in the moment, he also intends that our minds have a sense of a God-centered, heavenly priority, so that when tragedy comes, we are focused on the greater reward. I think Paul had this in mind when he said, "For this light momentary affliction is preparing for us an eternal weight of glory beyond all comparison" (2 Corinthians 4:17). And, instead of having our minds consumed by what's going on around us, Paul reminds us, "Set your minds on things that are above, not on things that are on earth" (Colossians 3:2). Having a God- and heaven-prioritized mindset will help us get through the sufferings we experience here on earth. This point will be further discussed in various places throughout this book, and specifically in Chapter 12.

Additionally, and possibly most importantly, the Bible is a sixty-six-book exposition of godly men and women experiencing tragedy and suffering, showing how they thought about these things in general and toward their specific situation, and how they think when tragedy and suffering has occurred or is imminent. I say this may be most important, because if our thoughts are ultimately responsible for how we handle tragedy, we want to learn how godly people thought *about* tragedy and *during* tragedy.

If you agree, our prayer should be something like this when we experience tragedy: "Lord, show me how to think about this situation that has happened to me." This is a good prayer, because thinking in a way that yields peace and hope instead of anxiety, depression, and anger during and following tragedy is very hard, even if we believe that God wants us to think a certain way about it. It's hard because of the cognitive pathways that have been created in our minds so far in our lives. Our current, limited cognitive pathways are the barriers that exist in our minds that keep us from overcoming our painful emotions and from living a life of peace and hope. This will be the focus of the next chapter.

Journal Questions

1. What tragedy or tragedies have you experienced in your life that you are having a hard time coping with? Be specific and detailed. Journaling about this is a way to prevent yourself from avoiding the memories, which could make coping even harder. Making it a practice to journal about the memories of your tragedy, rather than avoiding them, will help you learn to cope with your tragedy better.

2. What emotions do you feel when you think about your tragedy? Do you experience anxiety, depression, anger, or something else? Describe what this is like.

3. What do you think about the statements, "How we think affects how we feel" and "We can change how we feel by changing how we think"? Do you believe this is true? Has it been true for you? Describe an example of a time when your thoughts led you to have feelings of anxiety, depression, or anger.

4. I've stated that God's method for helping people through their tragedy and the difficult emotions that come with it has often been to do or say something that changes how they think. Can you think of a time when you were stuck in a difficult situation or feeling and God did or said something that helped your thinking, which led to you feeling differently about it? Start looking for ways that God is trying to help you think differently and write them in your journal.

5. In the last paragraph of this chapter, I asked us to pray, "Lord, show me how to think about this situation that has happened to me." I encourage you to pray this prayer every day until you find peace in your tragedy. Additionally, write down how you think God wants you to think about your tragic situation. Even if you don't currently think this way, write it down and ask God to help you to start thinking this way.

CHAPTER 2
Cognitive Pathways

One thing I miss about California, besides the weather and the beach, is the mountain ranges and hills. We lived in Orange County for a while and loved to hike. Here in Texas, there's hiking, but in my mind, *hiking* implies walking on a trail with some sort of incline. Most of Texas is flat. Either way, wherever you hike, when you are hiking, at least for us, we mostly stay on the trail or path. And even though there are no pavements, signs, curbs, or painted dotted lines, you know where the path is because it's been walked on a million times. On most hikes there is an obvious, dedicated, well-worn path.

But that path was not always there. It had to be created. Before the path, it was just like the rest of the area around you: forest, trees, bushes, rocks, or whatever. People repeatedly walking through that area created the path. It seems like it would not be easy to create one. At times when I've gone off the path, it's usually not easy to create a new one. You're treading through bushes, trees, and rocks. It can be fun, but it's not easy. In the movies, when someone is walking through a forest, they might be cutting through thick tree branches with a machete as they walk along. I've never done this, but it looks like a lot of work. Creating a pathway takes time and effort. But once it's created, it's easy to walk on.

A cognitive pathway is like this. As I am using the term, a *cognitive pathway* is a path in your mind that allows for a certain set of beliefs. We all have cognitive pathways. There are certain beliefs that are carved into our minds that, like the well-worn pathway on a hike, we've been down repeatedly. It's grooved into our minds and fixed, like a well-etched path through a forest. It feels easy, normal, comfortable, and safe. To go off this path in your mind, to add to it, or to take a completely different direction feels hard, abnormal, uncomfortable, and unsafe. So you remain on your path. And just like a pathway through a forest, it eventually stops. If you want to keep going, you need to get out your machete.

Just as a pathway through a forest is limited, in that it can only take you so far, cognitive pathways are also limited and can only take you so far. This is a problem if you want or need to go further. Sometimes you may need to go deeper into the forest than you ever thought you would want or need to go. But go there, you must. And to do that, you need to expand the path you're on or create a new one. Our cognitive pathways only extend as far our experiences and what we've learned will allow.

Cognitive Pathways and Christian Beliefs

Many people who were fortunate to have grown up in a Christian home experienced early Christian training from their parents and their church through things like bedtime prayers, family Bible devotionals, Sunday school, and youth ministries, in addition to godly character training and being taught how to handle difficult relationships and take on a Christian worldview. This kind of upbringing is the start of a good cognitive pathway toward God. This is what we are trying to do with our own children. However, the full revelation of God is not contained in children's devotions, stories, or picture Bibles, nor should it be.

A cognitive pathway we may have developed about God is that he is loving and merciful, so he wants good for his children. This is true, but then how do we explain all the pain and suffering in the world, including the pain and suffering experienced by Christians? Another cognitive pathway about God may be that he wants us to live a fruitful, blessed, and generous life. This may be true, but how do we understand our life when everything we know and cherish is taken away through tragedy? Another cognitive pathway about God is reflected in how we talk about God when it comes to tragedy. We say, "God is in control." But what does this mean, exactly, when willful, sinful people commit wretched evil against us?

The picture Bible we used with our children showed Noah on the ark with all the cute animals arranged two by two. It did not show the millions of men, women, and children clinging to the sides of the ark while they drowned in the worldwide flood. It showed David swinging his sling but did not show him cutting off Goliath's head with Goliath's sword. It showed Daniel petting the lions in the lions' den, but it did not show the men who were thrown in afterward and torn from limb to limb while being eaten alive. And thank goodness children's Bibles do not depict the slaughter of children, the rape of Dinah by her brother, the solicitation of prostitution by Judah, or the open incest between Absalom and his father's wife.

A child's young mind is not ready to handle many of the realities portrayed in Scripture or that exist in life. As I read my own Bible to my children when they were younger, I filtered and skipped over certain parts. Whether you agree with this strategy or not when it comes to raising children, I think we would agree that it would not be good for an adult to do this in their own spiritual development. An adult should read and understand the whole Bible. At some point, we need to move from milk to solid food (Hebrews 5:12–14).

Unfortunately, many of us stay on milk into adulthood. This may not be intentional. It may be due to poor training in the home we grew up in, a lack of emphasis, appreciation, and even exaltation of God's word in our church, or an overly busy schedule. In any case, I think there is a likelihood that adults on spiritual milk do not know or do not care that they are missing out on spiritually solid food. For the former, they don't know there are more, deeper, and richer truths in God's word to discover. For the latter, there is a lack of importance of God's word in their life. My point is not to judge the reason, just to say that many adults live on much less of God's word, virtue, and spiritual realities than they should, and they are becoming emaciated.

Many people also do not go deeper because they've never had to. There has never been a bear chasing them through the forest that forces them to take the path further or veer off to a new path in order to save their own life. Maybe the tragedy you are experiencing now is like nothing you have ever experienced before. That was the case for me, and for Sarah and Brittany, the women we discussed in Chapter 1. Their experiences were new for them, and tragedy to that magnitude was new for them. If you've never really suffered, don't be surprised if it's hard the first time through. You are going to get some cuts and bruises and soreness on this path. That's normal. You're treading through paths you've never been down before and exercising muscles you've never used before. It's going to hurt. But your options are to expand your pathway and save your life from the ferocious bear, or stay within the limits of your pathway and be mauled to death. This was my experience when I was diagnosed with MS.

Deeper into the Woods

One thing I've learned in conducting hundreds of clinical interviews over the last nearly twenty years is that most people don't have an equally hard life their entire life. They have ups and downs. Sure, there are people whose whole life seems like a bad country song, and the cloud of doom seems to follow them everywhere they go. But most people have some good times mixed in with the bad. And if they are seeing me, they have had some serious rough patches. Countless times, I have heard people describe a particular year, set of years, or period in their life that was especially difficult, when a lot of *stuff* happened. They lived to tell the story, but their tragedy left behind some scars. Sometimes deep ones. Sometimes multiple—that was my situation, literally, as I'll explain momentarily.

They say having a baby is one of the most stressful things that can happen in a person's life. The Holmes and Rahe Life Stress Inventory, also known as the Life Change Index Scale, lists 43 life events that can lead to stress, with each event accounting for a different score, all of which are added together for a total stress score. The American Institute of Stress says that scores between 150 and 300 predict a 50 percent chance of a health breakdown in the next two years. Scores above 300 have an 80 percent chance.[6] This can include a breakdown of physical or mental health.

It turns out that having a baby captures at least fifteen of the forty-three stressors listed on this inventory. To start, being pregnant is on the list (40 points), and having a baby is on the list (39 points). So, right off the bat, moms have seventy-nine points. For those moms and dads who have experienced this life-changing event, you know the stress isn't just for moms, and it doesn't stop there.

1. Personal illness *(mom gets morning sickness or postpartum depression)* – **53 points**

2. Change of health of a family member *(baby gets sick; parents aren't sleeping so their immune system is shot)* – **44 points**

3. Sexual difficulties *(yes, especially if mom is nursing!)* – **39 points**

4. Business readjustment *(yes, try doing things the exact same way after having a baby)* – **39 points**

5. Change in financial state *(do I need to explain this one?)* – **38 points**

6. Change to different line of work *(sometimes one spouse becomes a stay-at-home parent)* – **36 points**

7. Change in frequency of arguments *(this is what no sleep will do)* – **35 points**

8. Trouble with in-laws *(you'd be surprised at what having a baby will do to this relationship!)* – **29 points**

9. Change of living conditions *(have you seen what the house looks like after a week of a newborn living in it?)* – **25 points** *(should be more!)*

10. Revision of personal habits *(try going to the gym those first few months)* – **24 points**

11. Change in working hours or conditions *(for spouses working outside the home and for stay-at-home parents, we don't get a break!)* – **20 points**

12. Change in recreation *(yep)* – **19 points**

13. Change in social activities *(yep)* – **18 points**

14. Change in sleep habits *(I can't believe this is only worth 16 points!)* – **16 points**

15. Change in eating habits *(if you haven't had a baby, you don't get it)* – **15 points**

Total = 529 points

Seriously, 529 points! That's 229 points, or 76 percent, over the amount the American Institute of Stress says has an 80 percent chance of leading to a health breakdown. Even if you take out one or two of these, you're still well over 300. As you can see, having a baby leads to a lot of changes and a lot of stress. So it was for us.

My wife and I got married in 2003, the same time I started graduate school for psychology. It was a five-year academic program to receive a doctorate, not including internships. We decided to wait until I finished the doctorate to start trying to have kids. At the end of 2008, we were pregnant! I say "we," but my wife would beg to differ. Anyway, it was in May 2009 that our first son was born.

As if all the stress leading up to the delivery day wasn't enough, then I get the email that would change my life even more for the next year. It was May 15, 2009, the Friday before our son was born. I had just completed a 1,500-hour internship and was on my way to receiving full licensure as a psychologist in the state of California. We were eagerly awaiting confirmation from the California Board of Psychology that they had received and processed my internship hours so that I could move on to the next step.

I was relieved to have finished these hours. I was weary from making minimal income doing work I wasn't passionate about, and from weekly meetings with my supervisor. I was ready to move on. I had reached the finish line of this very important step. Mind you, this was the second half of 3,000 hours in total that I completed. The first half had been completed a year and a half earlier, so by this time we were beyond ready for it to be done.

My wife was very pregnant, and I was working from home that day when I received an email from the board stating that they had denied all 1,500 hours of my internship. I couldn't breathe. I read the email again. And again. Apparently, there was a discrepancy in how my supervisor and I signed and dated the form we sent the board to indicate the completion of hours. One signature and one date were wrong. Our bad. I thought, *"Well, we just need to fix it and send it back in."*

But like my favorite Netflix show, *Cobra Kai*, the board shows "No Mercy." Trying to get ahold of someone on a Friday afternoon was impossible, so I spent all weekend in agony. When I did talk to someone the following week, they were like, "This is the rule. Tough luck, kid." Got to love bureaucracy! My supervisor got involved and even talked with an attorney about suing the board. Even the attorney said there are no options and advised that I redo the internship. All 1,500 hours.

So, here we go. We're about to have a baby, and I'm still underpaid, still unlicensed, and with a mountain of student loan debt. No, they don't wait until you're working in your career to start collecting. Our son Christopher was born, and those first few months were magical and overwhelming at the same time. I wouldn't trade it for anything. But it was challenging. Especially since I'd never been around infants, changed a diaper, fed a baby, warmed up milk, or anything like that. For those of you who are veterans at having babies, I honor you. I knew lots of other guys who were in the same boat as I was and handling it about the same way, so I was rarely lonely in my pity party.

For whatever reason, around this time I started having intermittent painful tingling episodes in both of my hands. It felt like my hands were literally on fire and being poked with blazing hot needles. Painful, scary, and puzzling. My primary care physician referred me to a physical therapist to rule out a pinched nerve, then a hand specialist to rule out carpal tunnel syndrome, and finally, to a neurologist. After several weeks of MRIs, blood work, a spinal tap, and other testing, the diagnosis of MS was made. It was a relief to finally have a diagnosis, and it was a nightmare to learn that it was something serious. I had heard of MS but had no idea what it was.

MS is a neurological autoimmune disease that describes a condition in which a person's immune system attacks the protective covering surrounding their central nervous system, specifically the person's brain and spinal cord, leaving lesions, or scars, which are called *sclerosis. Multiple* means that there are more than one. A person can have a variety of physical symptoms, depending on what part of the brain or spinal cord the scars are located on. Symptoms can include fatigue; vision problems; muscle spasms; stiffness and weakness; mobility problems; pain; problems with thinking, learning, and planning; depression and anxiety; sexual problems; bladder problems; bowel problems; vertigo and dizziness; and speech and swallowing difficulties.

The problem with MS is that no one knows for sure what causes it, and there is no cure. The treatment is diet, lifestyle changes, and disease modifying drugs, which for me meant a daily injection of medication. The course and severity of the disease is unpredictable. My neurologist actually started crying in her office and told me that given my age, and that I'm male, my prognosis isn't good. I'm not usually the brightest guy in the room, but I know that when your neurologist is crying, this is not good! And this is not something a thirty-one-year-old man with a new baby, a wife who isn't working, a pile of debt, and a career that hasn't happened yet wants to hear.

Emotionally and spiritually, I was trying to *hang in there*. Anxiety, depression, and anger would come and go. I felt anxious over what would happen to me and my family. I felt depression and self-pity, and asked questions like, "Why did this happen to me?" I continued to imagine a dismal future with me disabled and unable to be the husband and father I wanted to be. I felt angry at God for letting this happen. I now know what was happening: My cognitive pathway only went so far. I just couldn't accept in my mind a God who would let me be disabled. Wait, a God who would *want* me to be disabled. A God who planned this from the foundation of the world, before anything came to be. A God who is perfect, who doesn't make mistakes, and is all-loving, all-wise, and all-powerful, yet who still allowed me to have MS and a future of painful disability. I kept shaking my head and saying, "No, this cannot be!"

But the *cannot* is from me. It's not in the Bible. There is no biblical precedent that would allow us to believe that Christians can't become disabled. My cognitive pathway stopped short of the realities portrayed in

Scripture, and I thought, *"Surely not I, Lord."* Yet doesn't this happen to most of us when tragedy strikes? Don't we think, *"Certainly, God couldn't* want *this to happen."* And we have a hard time getting our minds around a God who may want something for us that is contrary to what we would want for ourselves. Our tragedy is a reality that we don't want and never would have asked for or imagined, and a reality that we don't think we can live with.

Prosperity, Really?

The prosperity gospel, in a nutshell, says that God wants us all to be healthy, wealthy, and prosperous. It basically teaches that sickness, poverty, hardship, or failure in Christians occurs due to a lack of faith. Prosperity preachers have taken a few texts in isolation and out of context to create this doctrine, which contradicts the message of the Bible, including the cross of our Lord. The prosperity gospel is unbiblical and dangerous. But I think that I, and many others, have this prosperity narrative in the back of our minds. Sure, we may not believe the prosperity gospel in total, but lurking in the back of our minds is the thought that God sure does want us to prosper and not to suffer. Or, that God wouldn't allow his faithful servant to experience something horrific, something tragic.

We might say, "God wants me to be happy, and I can't be happy with (or without) _____." And we have in our minds this idea that if we are faithful to God, he is going to give it to us and put a divine hedge around us to shield us from tragedy. We think that God's blessings mean that life will go a certain way or that we'll have certain things in life. And we quote scriptures like Psalm 37:4, "Delight yourself in the Lord, and he will give you the desires of your heart" and Psalm 1:3, "He is like a tree planted by streams of water that yields its fruit in its season, and its leaf does not wither. In all that he does, he prospers."

But before we play divine referee and call foul on God, it would be helpful to remember the following history, recorded in the Bible, of people who suffered great tragedy:

1. Joseph was sold into slavery by his brothers who hated him and loved money. Then he was falsely accused of rape and put in jail for years.

2. The Israelites were ruthlessly oppressed as slaves by their Egyptian taskmasters.

3. Israelite moms and dads experienced the judicial extermination of their sons at least twice in history, once while slaves in Egypt, and once when oppressed by Roman rule.

4. David spent at least a decade of his life on the run from Saul, who wanted to kill him. Then his son died as an infant, his daughter was raped by one of his other sons, and another son tried to kill him and take over the kingdom.

5. Job's ten children were killed in bad weather when a roof collapsed on them. He was then afflicted with detestable and excruciating sores all over his body and other horrible symptoms such that he wanted to die.

6. Jeremiah was persecuted for his entire ministry life and charged with treason. On one occasion, he was locked up in a sewer to die. He was released, but tradition holds that he was later stoned to death.

7. John the Baptist was imprisoned and then beheaded at the request of a teenage girl so that a sinful monarch could impress his friends.

8. Extrabiblical writings suggest that all twelve apostles were murdered, except John, who was put on an island for criminals where he eventually died.

9. Stephen was stoned to death by religious leaders.

10. Jesus himself was persecuted during his entire ministry life, and then was sold out by one of his closest friends, abandoned by his other close friends, hated and rejected by his own people, and then mocked, tortured, and crucified by pagans.

Given this list, is there anything that could happen to you or me such that we could then legitimately say, "This cannot be" or that we could argue with God about? Tragedy happens to faithful, God-fearing Christians all the time. We are not always shielded from it. Does your cognitive pathway extend to the point where you can experience a tragedy and not become bitter at God, or fall into a serious clinical depression or anxiety that is unrelenting and leaves you stuck and unfunctional? Does your cognitive pathway keep God on his throne during tragedy? In other words, does your thinking allow for a God who could permit or even be the cause of certain tragedies in your life?

How would you think about God if someone broke into your house in the middle of the night and murdered your whole family in front of you? Or if a suicide bomber killed fifty people next to you in a crowded stadium? Or if your daughter were raped? Or if your ten-year-old son developed cancer and died? Or if your teenage son committed suicide? Or if your two-year-old daughter drowned in your pool? Or if your spouse of twenty-five years left you with three children to take care of? Or if he or she cheated on you with your best friend? Or if your child were born with a lifelong disability that required constant care? Or if a tsunami killed your wife while she was serving as a missionary, as the Indian Ocean Tsunami killed 225,000 men, women, and children in 2004?

These are tragedies that happen in this world, and some of them happen every day. Our cognitive pathway has got to extend to the point where God stays on his throne during all this. This means that we could have a God who is all-powerful and all-loving, yet still have any one of these things happen to us. We need to be able to see God in control of all events and circumstances under the sun. Doing so will bring more emotional stability in times of chaos and calamity than believing that God is not in control of these things. God is in control of tragedy. Do you believe this?

Cognitive Pathways and God

One of my favorite movie series of all time is *The Matrix*. In part one of the four-part series, the lead character, Neo, played by Keanu Reeves, is stuck in the matrix, a virtual reality that functions as a reality for all who are in it. However, in actuality, it's more like a dream. All who are in it are asleep, have been asleep all their lives, and are controlled by artificial intelligence (AI). In the movie, there are characters who have escaped the matrix, and whose job it is to rescue others. One of their missions is to find "the One" who can save the whole world from the power of AI and destroy the matrix.

The group of rescuers, led by the character Morpheus, enter the matrix to save Neo, whom they believe is the One. In this unforgettable scene, Morpheus challenges Neo to make a choice: Stay in the virtual reality of the matrix forever, or leave the matrix to enter reality forever. These choices are represented by a blue pill (stay in the matrix) and a red pill (leave the matrix). Really, it's a choice to continue to stay in dream world and believe a lie, or escape the lie and believe and live in the truth. It's a choice of continued slavery or freedom. We know what happens. Neo takes the red pill and escapes the matrix. He chooses to let go of the lie that he's been made to believe all his life. He chooses to be set free.

Most of our modern, secular world today lives in a type of matrix, a virtual reality that says God doesn't exist, but if he does exist, he's a passive God, uninvolved in the day-to-day affairs of this world. At best, this matrix allows for a God who made the world, gave it a good spin, and is now sitting back and watching it go. The God of this matrix doesn't govern the tragedies in this world. It's not that he doesn't want to. He can't. Humans, and Satan for that matter, are too much of a wild card. God couldn't have stopped Hitler, bin Laden, or the man in my home state who, on May 24, 2022, killed nineteen children and two teachers at Robb Elementary School in Uvalde, Texas. In this matrix, God is sad and angry, but mostly frustrated because his hands are tied.

The God of this matrix is either unable or unwilling. If unable, he's simply doing his best given the mess he has to work with. If unwilling, well, then he's evil. More evil than Hitler, bin Laden, and the hundreds of men and women who have committed atrocities like the shooter at Robb

Elementary School, put together. If I have the power to stop a crime, let's say, a rape, and I look the other way, wouldn't that make me about as bad as the rapist? If God has the power to stop all crime and other tragedy, but doesn't, where does that put God? We, in our matrix, would say that God must be unwilling because he's evil, meaning that he intends evil for evil purposes. What if God intends evil, not for evil purposes, but for good purposes? Does intention matter? If we don't have an answer to these questions, we will likely shake our fist at God when tragedy strikes.

Thankfully, this matrix is not reality. It is one integrated, colossal lie from Satan, the deceiver of the whole world (Revelation 12:9). And he has many of us fooled. Fooled into believing that God either doesn't exist, lacks authority, or doesn't care. But like those in *The Matrix* movie who are unwitting victims of the virtual reality they live in, many of us are in the same boat. We have been fed this lie our entire lives, so we don't know anything different. Therefore, we are unconscious to the God-centered reality we live in. This book, and many others like it, stand at the door and knock with a red pill in hand. Take the red pill! Escape the lie that says God doesn't exist, lacks authority, or doesn't care. Escape the lie that says God can allow tragedy but never cause it. Escape the lie that says God never wills suffering.

If you are experiencing ongoing, chronic negative emotions like anxiety, depression, or anger following a tragic experience, it is likely that your cognitive pathway falls short of a God-centered reality. If you are experiencing this, I do not have a negative judgment for you. I was there at one point too. We've got to fight to see things from a different perspective. To move through the hell that you are now living in, you must develop or expand your cognitive pathway to think about God differently. If you are stuck, it is likely that your current concepts about God are not enough to get you through it. Your cognitive pathway has likely led you to a false or incomplete representation of God, resulting in a God in your mind who is too small, resulting in complete emotional wreckage following your tragedy.

In the next chapter, we will focus on expanding our cognitive pathway to be able to accept and find peace with the tragedies that have occurred in our lives. This will require thinking differently—specifically, thinking differently about God and tragedy. Often, the situation you are going through, or have been through, can't be fixed. There is no solution. There is no answer. There is no way out, only *through*. You can't change it. The only thing, absolutely the only thing you can do, is to change how you think about it. Emotional healing following tragedy requires a different way of thinking than you have been doing. We will develop a cognitive pathway toward a God-centered reality, one that acknowledges and embraces the almighty God of the universe, "who is over all and through all and in all" (Ephesians 4:6), including *all tragedies* in the universe.

To do this will require hard work, an open mind, and considering some things you may have never considered before. There is some theology to address. But, as I have said, this is not a theology book. It's a self-help book for Christians who are struggling with emotional pain during or following a tragedy. However, good theology is therapeutic. We simply can't expect to have stable mental health in this chaotic world without a solid biblical framework by which to see God, the world, and our tragedy. So please hang in there with me as we dive deeper into this complex discussion. The next chapter may be the most difficult one in this book to conceptually grasp, but after that, the rest is pretty straightforward. Tragedy requires you to go deeper down the cognitive pathway, deeper than you would have gone without it. Let's continue on this path together.

Journal Questions

1. Describe a cognitive pathway that you have about God that you feel may be inaccurate or not quite on point. How does this affect how you see God when tragedy strikes, and how does this affect how you see your tragedy?

2. Have you been living on spiritual milk, rather than on solid spiritual food? How has this affected how you think and feel when tragedy strikes?

3. Are you holding on to a "prosperity narrative"? If your cognitive pathways about God fall short of the God-centered reality of the Bible and universe we live in, admit that you are living in a sort

of secular matrix. How can you come out of this? How can you escape this matrix and live in reality?

4. I described how my tragedy of being diagnosed with MS caused me to go "deeper into the woods." Describe how your tragedy has done the same for you.

5. How can living from a deeper spiritual reality help you when tragedy strikes?

CHAPTER 3
Going Deeper

I'll begin this chapter by reminding us what a cognitive pathway is. A cognitive pathway, as I am using the term, is a path in our mind that allows for a certain set of beliefs. I use the word *pathway*, or *path*, because I think that it accurately describes what I am trying to communicate. It's like a walkway in our mind that leads us to a conclusion. That conclusion can be helpful or unhelpful, biblically accurate or inaccurate, correctly or incorrectly aligned with reality. Or it can lie somewhere between any of these points.

If the word *pathway* doesn't help you or doesn't make sense to you, then think about what I am trying to describe as a set of beliefs. A way of seeing the world. The way you perceive reality. Simply describing it as a set of beliefs or a way of seeing or perceiving the world is fine. It's just that in our lives, when something happens, we take a little mental walk down a mental lane. That mental lane is filled with things like "If this, then that" statements, assumptions, and predictions that lead to a particular conclusion on a matter: the end of the road. Then usually, if our "If this, then that" statements, assumptions, and predictions were right, we end up in a good mental and emotional spot. If not, we could end up stuck. And by *stuck*, I mean confused, discouraged, hopeless, anxious, depressed, or angry. This is not a good place to be.

Let me give you a real-life example. I was working with a particular client who, every week, came in with a new disaster to discuss. Seriously, it was like he chose the "bad luck card" every morning before coffee and kept it with him all day until bedtime. Not trivial stuff either. His car broke down. He got COVID. His boss was being unreasonable. He got a speeding ticket. He had a leak in his roof during a major storm that damaged his living room. He lost his phone. His wife had a major health crisis and needed surgery. He started getting calls from his daughter's teacher about behavior problems in class. And more, and more.

As he took the walk down his mental lane, or cognitive pathway, he thought (and said) things like, "Such and such happened to me; the world must be out to get me" ("If this, then that" statement), "God must be angry at me, and I'm being punished" (assumption), and "My life will never get better" (prediction). What do you think this guy felt when thinking like this? He felt a great deal of anxiety, depression, and anger that was hard to shake.

This man's cognitive pathway, or set of beliefs, led him down a path of thinking that ended in a bad spot for him. And since he's married with children, a bad spot for them as well, as they have to live with him. What was wrong here? On the measure of helpful or unhelpful, biblically accurate or inaccurate, and correctly or incorrectly aligned with reality, his cognitive pathway leaned toward unhelpful, biblically inaccurate, and incorrectly aligned with reality. That's not to say that everything he was thinking was on this end of the measure. But the general narrative of the cognitive pathway he was on was mostly unhelpful, mostly biblically inaccurate, and mostly incorrectly aligned with reality, which was why he was anxious, depressed, and angry.

There are two possibilities when we are stuck, as this man was: The first is that our cognitive pathways are too limited, in that what and how we think needs to be expanded upon. For most people, our cognitive pathways are just limited and need expansion. Or better, too shallow and need more depth. The other possibility is that the cognitive pathway is entirely off, and we need a new one.

For the former, much of what we think is helpful, biblically accurate, and correctly aligned with reality, but it falls short, or is incomplete. For the latter, we have some seriously wrong beliefs that need correction. But why is this important? Why are cognitive pathways so important to us? As you can see, what and how we think plays a huge part in how we feel. A pathway that stops short or a pathway that is going in the wrong direction both lead to feelings that are undesired. This is not to say that once your cognitive pathway is expanded or corrected you will have no undesirable emotions. It's just that your emotions will have less control over you and will be less devasting, and you'll be able to manage them better.

Searching for Resolution

Our cognitive pathways about God, tragedy, and suffering are very important. The correct and complete pathway is not automatically downloaded into our brains when we become Christians. Often, we have been taught some false or incorrect things about God, tragedy, and suffering, or we have never really had to think about these topics before. Sometimes it takes experiencing a tragedy and suffering to start thinking about them. How we understand God in light of our tragedy and suffering can affect how we perceive and feel about the tragedy and suffering we are experiencing. It can also affect how we feel about God, others, ourselves, and the world around us.

Specifically, for most of the Christians that I have encountered who have experienced a tragedy and are therefore suffering, the cognitive pathway in their mind that needs to be developed has to do with understanding and accepting God's involvement in their tragedy. Typically, tragedies fall into one or more of these four categories: death, disease, disaster, and despicable evil. Often, when a Christian experiences one or more of these, they struggle to understand God's involvement in and with their tragedy. They ask questions like the following:

- "Where was God when this happened?"

- "Why did God let this happen?"

- "If God is so powerful, why didn't he stop this?"

- "If God is so loving, why would he let me suffer like this?"

People with unresolved questions like this can become emotionally unstable. I've seen it a million times. My attempt in this chapter is to expand our cognitive pathways a bit so that we can begin to resolve some of these questions and gain a better footing for emotional stability. Notice that I said "resolve." I did not say "answer." Resolving a dilemma is different from answering it. We may not have exact answers to all our specific questions. Reality is not always black and white. But it's less gray than many make it out to be. There are ways to understand tragedy that will bring resolution to our minds and hearts. Resolution is like a settling in our mind, even a settling about knowing enough but not knowing everything. This is what I think we can achieve, and this achievement can reach milestones toward our emotional healing.

In expanding our cognitive pathways toward a deeper understanding of God, suffering, and tragedy, I have Colossians 1:9–10 in mind:

> And so, from the day we heard, we have not ceased to pray for you, asking that you may be filled with the knowledge of his will in all spiritual wisdom and understanding, so as to walk in a manner worthy of the Lord, fully pleasing to him: bearing fruit in every good work and increasing in the knowledge of God.

I hope that this chapter will help to fill you with the knowledge of his will in spiritual wisdom and understanding, and that you will increase in the knowledge of God.

All Means All

Several years ago, Texas Hold'em poker became really popular, and I went to several men's poker nights with a bunch of the guys in our church. I don't advocate or even like gambling. Even when we played, I think we had a $5 buy-in, just to keep it interesting. And that would be for the whole night. It was more about the game and hanging out with the guys. But something I remember is when players used to go all in. *All in*, in poker, means that you put all your chips into the pot, hoping to either beat everyone's hand, or that all the players fold instead of having to match your bet. When someone said, "I'm all in," they pushed all their chips, sometimes stacks of them, into the middle of the table. They pushed *all* their chips to the center. They couldn't say, "I'm all in" and hold some back. You'd get shanked at some poker tables for pulling that nonsense! *All* means all.

If a cashier gets robbed at gunpoint and the robber says, "Give me all the money in the cash register," the cashier should probably not try to give the robber some of the money in the cash register. *All* means all.

When my son was twelve, he had a hamster that he kept in a cage in his room. To clean the cage, he would take it into the backyard. Gross, right? But it's better than in the house. And hamster cages stink after a few days, so he did it twice a week. He knew that his job was not complete until he cleaned up all the hamster-cage bedding that ended up on the ground instead of in the trash bag. When he came inside and told me he was done, like a good dad, I checked his work. Of course, there was still some hamster-cage bedding on the ground. What did I tell him? Like a good dad, I said, "*All* means all."

This is not complicated. It's not supposed to be. We make things complicated when we start saying, "Does *all* really mean all?" Yes, it does. Let's not try to find exceptions and exclusions. We sometimes do this with the Bible.

When the Apostle Paul in Romans 11:36 said, "From him and through him and to him are all things," I don't think he meant all things except suicide bombers in crowded malls, stillborn babies, or politicians who lie. When he said in Ephesians 1:11 that God "works all things according to the counsel of his will," I don't think he meant all things except cancer, earthquakes, and people who slander you on the internet. And when he said in Colossians 1:16–17, "By him all things were created, in heaven and on earth, visible and invisible, whether thrones or dominions or rulers or authorities—all things were created through him and for him. And he is before all things, and in him all things hold together," I don't think he meant all things except housing market crashes, car accidents, and your husband who left because he wasn't "happy." *All* means all.

For people who believe in God, it's easy for us to believe that God governs the natural elements of the universe. Planets rotating around the sun, the sun burning at around 10,000 degrees Fahrenheit, and asteroids colliding are all directed by God. The same with snow, hail, rain, thunder, and lightning on the earth. All are controlled by the mighty hand of

God. I really don't know many Christians who would argue that God is not involved in these occurrences. But Psalm 135:6, which says, "Whatever the Lord pleases, he does, in heaven and on earth, in the seas and all deeps" stretches beyond just the natural elements of the universe. It's like the children's song, "He's Got the Whole World in His Hands." Oh yes, he does. And even more than we thought.

Thinking about God

The Bible deals with massive amounts of death, disease, disaster, and despicable evil. The question is: Is God in control of all this, or are we the victims of chance, nature, randomness, the power of Satan, or the selfish and sinful desires of people? What kind of control does God have? Would God ever *will* tragedy? Would God ever will sin? If so, how does he will that sin happens without himself being a sinner? We will try to bring some resolution to these questions. As we go through this, keep in mind that there is an entire section of this book devoted to understanding the four main tragedies listed in the first sentence of this paragraph and God's involvement in them.

Where do we get our thoughts and ideas about God? Is it from songs, nature, or how we feel? Or how about from other people (e.g., what our parents taught us, what we read in books, what we see in movies, etc.)? Thoughts and ideas about God are everywhere. As a Christian, I believe that our thoughts and ideas about God should come from the Bible, the true word of God and the ultimate authority for truth regarding the person and nature of God. This is not to say that the other sources of knowledge I mentioned are wrong. It's just that they need to be checked against the Bible. The Bible has the final say on the matter. If you don't believe this, then what I say in this chapter, and possibly this whole book, will be difficult to accept.

I believe that the Bible puts forward God, who is running the entire universe, and specifically, the world we live in. Like a CEO of a massive corporation, God is calling the shots. Except unlike a CEO, God doesn't have a board of directors to seek counsel or get approval from. God consults the counsel of his own will (Ephesians 1:11) and doesn't need approval from anyone when he operates (Psalm 115:3). But what if

I am wrong? What if it's not true that God runs the universe, including the world we live in? What would the other options be? Maybe no one is running it? Maybe everything is random, happening by chance, or is the result of natural processes? Or maybe Satan is running the show? It sure seems like it sometimes.

In saying that God is running the entire universe, and specifically, the world we live in, I am including all tragedies that happen in this world, including the sinful choices of humans and the influence of Satan that cause so many of the tragedies and suffering. God decisively governs all that happens here, including evil, tragedies, and suffering. But what if we didn't believe this? Consider the following eight options of what you would have to believe about God in relation to evil, tragedy, and suffering if you did not believe this. There may be some overlaps here, but this will give you an idea of what we're left with if we don't believe that God governs the universe and everything that happens in it:

1. God is not real. There is no God. If there were a God, there would not be this much evil, tragedy, and suffering in the world. *This is the default belief of many atheists. They just don't get past this point. They can't imagine a world where the God of the Bible exists when they see the massive amount of evil, tragedy, and suffering in the world.*

2. God is real, he cares about us, and he is deeply bothered by the evil, tragedy, and suffering he sees in the world but isn't powerful enough to stop it. God and Satan share equal power and are up there duking it out. Sometimes God wins and sometimes Satan wins. God hates evil, tragedy, and suffering, but there's nothing he can do about it. *This paints the picture of a very frustrated God who wants to help us; he's doing his best, but it's not enough.*

3. God is real and is powerful enough to stop evil, tragedy, and suffering, but he doesn't care enough to do anything about it. He created the world and gave it a good spin, but now he sits

on his throne, watching from above, without intervening in our lives. *I don't know many people who believe this one.*

4. God is powerful enough to stop evil, tragedy, and suffering, but he will not override human free will. So, in a sense, he chooses to withhold his power to stop evil, tragedy, and suffering in order to preserve human free will. Evil, tragedy, and suffering can never be thwarted, redirected, or changed when humans will it. Evil, tragedy, and suffering are never God's will, they are only the will of humans and Satan. *It seems like most people believe this one, or something like it.*

5. God is more powerful than Satan, but Satan can ask "permission" from God to "allow" him (Satan) to cause suffering. God sometimes gives permission and sometimes does not. When God does give permission for evil, tragedy, and suffering, it was not his original intent. It was not planned, purposeful, or in the mind of God before Satan requested it. When Satan requested it, God must have deemed it good, and so gave permission. But the fact is, God did not intend for the evil, tragedy, and suffering to happen in the first place.

6. God is all-powerful and all-loving, but he doesn't know what is going to happen, and he doesn't have a plan. He reacts to what happens and is able to work good into it for Christians. Satan is a wild card. God doesn't have a leash on this monster, and so suffering is random, unplanned, and meaningless.

7. God knows what is going to happen, because he sees the future, like a fortuneteller or a master chess player who knows the next move. God has a plan, one that is not followed because of human free will, and rather than intrude on our free will, he watches things happen, and then works good into it for Christians. We humans can mess up God's plan, and he must make alternate plans for us (i.e., a Plan B).

8. God governs the world, and only sinful people suffer. If you have experienced evil, tragedy, and suffering, you must have open or hidden sin. Evils, tragedies, and suffering are punishment by God toward sinners. God wants us all to be healthy, wealthy, and prosperous and will bless us with these things when we repent and have faith in him.

There are many theological debates here. My intention is not to overwhelm your mind with these options or go through each one of them. It's just to point out that this is what we are left with when we don't believe that God governs the entire world, including evil, tragedy, and suffering. As a psychologist, I look at this list and conclude that there is no way to experience relief from anxiety, depression, or anger following evil, tragedy, and suffering while believing any of these. All of them create a reality where God is not in ultimate control. If God is not in ultimate control of the evils, tragedies, and sufferings of the world, then we have much reason to be anxious, depressed, and angry. We are hanging in the balance, dangling over a sea of uncertainty, instability, and doubt. We are left to ourselves, subject to either the randomness and unpredictability of humans, nature, or chance—or worse, we are hapless victims against the most powerful demon that has ever existed. Who could find any peace or security in this?

But take a walk down a different cognitive pathway with me. We are not hanging in the balance. Rather, we have our feet on a secure rock of stability, a foundation that is certain and trustworthy. For some of us, this may be a new way of thinking about God, evil, tragedy, and suffering, a new way of seeing the world: that God is in control of all the evil, tragedy, and suffering there is. We have used the phrase *in control* in this book. No doubt you have heard it when something bad happens. "God is in control," they say. But what does this mean? I use the phrase *God is in control*, because that is the phrase we often quote or say to explain tragedy, and if meant and used right, I think it represents reality. But the phrase itself doesn't really explain anything. It just brings up more questions. What do we mean by "God is in control" when our spouse dies of cancer, a school building collapses and kills several children, or commercial airplanes are hijacked and used as weapons? A deeper understanding of this, and a firmer foundation in this reality, will help us gain emotional stability in times of tragedy.

God Is in Control

We can't discuss the severest types of tragedy without first understanding what is meant by *God is in control*. This phrase is used in our society, often by well-meaning Christians who want to encourage someone who has experienced great loss. We tell it to ourselves to calm our anxious thoughts and give ourselves hope. And I do believe it is true, but I must explain what I mean. Otherwise, as I said, it really does trigger more questions than answers. Did God *make* someone choose to plan and carry out an explosion in a crowded mall? Or by *control*, do we mean that God chose to allow it to happen? Did God make a choice regarding this incident at all? Did God decide for the infant to die in his mother's womb, cancer to grow in an otherwise healthy eighteen-year-old, or for my boss twenty-one years ago to fire me for being unwilling to lie in my sales calls? By *control*, does that mean God makes it happen? Or because he's in control, does that mean he could have stopped it, but instead allowed it to happen? Or maybe it means that it would have been much worse if God were *not* in control. If none of the eight options in the prior section adequately explain God's control, then what does?

When I say, "God is in control" what do I mean? Think about what you would mean if you said someone was in control of a vehicle. You would mean that the person in the driver's seat is holding the steering wheel, using the gas and brake petals, and, if the car has manual transmission, shifting gears according to the speed of the vehicle. And you would mean that the driver is doing all these things to direct the vehicle where they want it to go. The driver is in control of the vehicle, deciding or determining where to go (e.g., when and where to turn and whether to go faster or slower or to stop). The person in the passenger's seat is not in control of the vehicle, but rather, is only a passenger, going where the driver decides. The passenger may request or even demand that the driver drive a certain way or go to a certain place, but the decision to acquiesce to the passenger's request or demand is still up to the driver. The driver, in control of the vehicle, decides how to operate the vehicle and where to go.

In the mid-2000s, famous country singer Carrie Underwood performed a song on the hit television show *American Idol* called "Jesus, Take the Wheel." The song is about a young mom whose car spins out of control while she is driving on Christmas Eve with her baby in the back seat. When the car comes to a stop, and the mom realizes that she and her baby are both safe, she reflects on what just happened and how in her life, she has been trying to do it all on her own. She's distressed and overwhelmed, not just about the near-fatal accident, but about her life. She reasons that it's because she hasn't let Jesus be in the driver's seat of her life. So, "for the first time in a long time," she bows her head to pray and declares, "Jesus, take the wheel. Take it from my hands. 'Cause I can't do this on my own. I'm letting go." This song spent six weeks at the number one position on Billboard Hot Country Songs and sold over 2.7 million copies in the United States.

I get it. I understand that in life, we often try to manage, or take control, of our own lives, and we resist God's direction and help. We rebel against God's commands for our lives and think we can do it on our own. If our life is a vehicle, we take the wheel, and we go and do whatever we want, instead of letting Jesus drive. I like the song, but I hate to break it to Carrie Underwood fans: Jesus had the wheel the whole time. He's been in control of the vehicle for your entire life. It's like when I did driver training at fifteen years old. I don't know if they still do it like this, but the car I was in had a steering wheel, a brake petal, and a gas pedal on the passenger's side. I remember trying to get on a highway too slowly, and the trainer floored it. With all the controls in front of me in the driver's seat, I had some options, but I knew who was really in control of the vehicle.

Jesus doesn't let go of our lives. Even when we rebel, he patiently guides the vehicle toward the destination where he wants it to go. Here is a summary explanation that I have written, after a lot of reading and thinking, about the reality of God, evil, tragedy, and suffering described in the Bible:

> God governs the entire world. Everything that happens, including evil tragedies and sufferings, happens according to his *planned will*. God either directly causes or permits everything that happens. If it is by permission, it is

a "planned permission,"[7] planned before the world ever began. Nothing takes God by surprise. God is all-loving and all-powerful. He *uses* the sinful inclinations of people's hearts to accomplish his divine purposes, while himself remaining free from evil. Sometimes the sinful desires and inclinations of people's hearts result in real tragedy toward God's servants, but when this happens, it is by the express plan and purposes of God. No person is innocent of the evil they do, because they are acting in line with their own evil inclinations. But God *directs* or *allows* those evil inclinations to accomplish actions that in turn accomplish his ultimate purposes. And because God is all-loving and all-powerful, any evil tragedies or suffering that come upon a Christian are for the ultimate good of the Christan and, more importantly, the ultimate glorification of God.

I believe that this explanation represents the reality of God in a world of evil, tragedy, and suffering as described in the Bible, and gives full cause for finding meaning in any amount of suffering. Said another way, all suffering is meaningful. Nothing painful that you or I will ever go through in this life is meaningless. By meaningful, I mean that suffering is purposeful, and accomplishes, or aims to accomplish, something of value in your life that could not have been present without the suffering. Section IV of this book will examine this reality in greater detail. The explanation about God in relation to tragedies, especially evil tragedies, presented above, if believed and embraced, has a greater potential to reduce anxiety, depression, and anger, and to produce peace, hope, and contentment in a believer, compared to the eight presented earlier in this chapter, since this is the only explanation that describes God as fully in control of the evil tragedies and sufferings in this world. All the others put shackles on God. This explanation describes a fully capable God who loves us and is in control of all things, and who keeps us on the solid rock of certainty, and not dangling in the balance.

Does God Control People?

At this point, you may be asking, "Does God control people?" My answer is no, God does not control people. Everyone who sins or performs a righteous deed from a heart of faith does so from the preferences of their heart. They either really want to sin, or they really want to obey God. That they would really want to sin is the natural preference of all people, unless God intervenes in their life, giving them a heart of faith (Ezekiel 36:26–27; 2 Corinthians 4:6; Ephesians 2:1–8). So, when someone's sin causes tragedy in our life, that person is acting within their natural, sinful tendencies and is therefore fully accountable before God. They have not been *made* to do evil; they *want* to do evil. It's fully within their preferences. Only if God moves their preferences would they choose anything else. And God uses the sinful preferences of people to accomplish his divine purposes. We echo Joseph, who said to his brothers, "You meant evil against me, but God meant it for good" (Genesis 50:20). While Joseph's brothers meant their sinful actions for evil, God meant their sinful actions for good. This scripture, which can be proclaimed by anyone who has experienced an evil tragedy, and this topic in general, will be expounded on later in this book.

If we experience a tragedy that is a result of someone's evil behavior, we can be confident that, while the person acting within their own sinful preferences did so for their own evil reasons, God has different reasons for the evil actions. The person is 100 percent accountable before God for their actions, and God has used the sinful person's actions to accomplish his will. The sinful person who caused tragedy was an instrument in God's hand to bring about God's purposes, which are sometimes good and restorative and sometimes for discipline or punishment (consider Isaiah 10:5–15 for the latter). For Christians, we can know that, while the knife in the Master Surgeon's hand hurts us as he is cutting, the ultimate purpose of his knife is to cut the cancer out and bring healing. By faith, we believe that the tragedy caused by the sinful person is being used in the hand of God to accomplish good for us. This gives us peace in the face of evil tragedies.

In Section III, we will further consider God's control in the major tragedies we experience: death, disease, disaster, and despicable evil. The next section of this book, "Finding Peace in Our Feelings," deals with the most common emotions, or feelings, when going through tragedy, specifically, anxiety, depression, and anger. In these chapters, we'll take a closer look at each of these emotions, or feelings, in greater detail.

Journal Questions

1. Have you ever thought that you could be resolved about something without having all the answers? Can you learn to be comfortable with not knowing everything? How does it make you feel to not have an answer to everything? How can you work on being resolved even if you don't have all the answers?

2. How do you feel about Paul's statement in Ephesians 1:11, that God "works all things according to the counsel of his will"? Do you believe that all things, including all tragedies, are worked according to the counsel of God's will? If so, how does believing this help you cope with your tragedy?

3. What do you think about the eight incorrect or incomplete descriptions of God in relation to tragedy that were presented in this chapter? Do you believe any of them? If so, does your belief help you cope with your tragedy, or does it make coping more difficult?

4. If the summary I wrote about how God governs the entire universe is true, then all suffering is meaningful. Think deeply about how your suffering has been meaningful to you or in the lives of those around you. If you find it helpful, create a list of the ways that your suffering has been meaningful.

5. Finding meaning in our suffering is a great way to battle feelings of anxiety, depression, and anger. Decide today to battle your distressing feelings over your suffering with the belief that all suffering is meaningful. Refer to, and pray through, your list of "meaning" that you wrote in journal question #4 above.

Section II:
Finding Peace in
Our Feelings

CHAPTER 4

Anxiety

L isa is a forty-five-year-old married woman with three children, ages seventeen, fifteen, and thirteen. She married James right out of college, twenty-three years ago. They are devout members of their local church and involved in their children's youth ministry. James works full time in sales, supporting his family, while Lisa is mostly a stay-at-home mom, though she has a small online business selling homemade jewelry. A typical day for Lisa includes preparing meals for her family, organizing and managing the home and their children's busy schedules, and making jewelry to sell online. James and Lisa are very hospitable, regularly having other families in their home, and they have several friends.

James and Lisa did not grow up in Christian homes. Both sides are divorced. Lisa's mom and stepdad are involved in her life, while James's relationship with his mom is minimal. Though he has tried to connect with her over the years, it's been mostly one-sided, with James making the most effort. James's dad died ten years ago from health complications related to alcohol abuse. James and Lisa's children are good students, involved in sports, respectful to adults, and have lots of friends in and out of the church.

Lisa has struggled with anxiety all her life, thinking she is never doing enough and is never good enough. This overachieving, perfectionistic mentality has been the source of much of her stress, often causing sleep-minimal nights and overloading of her schedule so that she's late all the time and doesn't finish tasks. A good day for Lisa is when she accomplishes everything on her to-do list. This doesn't happen often, which of course feeds her narrative that she is never good enough, which leads her to feeling depressed. All this she learned from her parents. Growing up, Lisa's parents were constantly nagging her to do more and do better. They were never satisfied. While Lisa has talked about this in detail with her therapist and is aware of her tendencies and how they originated, old habits are hard to break.

James and Lisa have had a decent relationship over the years. From the outside they look great. Lisa has made sure of that. On the inside, there is arguing, especially when James drinks too much. Alcohol has been a problem for him. Being in sales, he often entertains clients and uses this as an excuse when he overdoes it. Though even when he is at home, he overdoes it. James is a life-of-the-party kind of guy, enjoying being the center of attention, and he is really liked by most people. He has a hard time "sitting still" and takes on more and more work, and work-travel opportunities, which keeps him away from home a lot of the time.

One night, out of nowhere, James announced to Lisa that he had a girlfriend and was leaving. He had been cheating on Lisa with his girlfriend for the past six months and was moving in with her. He had set up a separate bank account, and his paychecks would be directed there starting the following pay period. James told Lisa he'd send her money so she could pay the mortgage, but said he intended to sell the house as soon as possible. James didn't want custody of the children or an arranged schedule to see them; he said he'd see them when he could. He told Lisa it was up to her whether she filed for divorce, but he was leaving and not coming back. Lisa was on her own, with three kids.

For several days, Lisa was in shock and disbelief. Everyone was. James would not sit down with their pastor or friends to talk about what was going on. He completely shut everyone out. Lisa was having frequent panic attacks. She was restless and irritable, and couldn't sleep. She just couldn't believe what was happening. Dozens of questions ran through her mind: *"Why did this happen?" "What am I going to do?" "How will the kids handle this?" "Will the kids and I be ok?" "Was it my fault?" "What will people think?"* These questions and more flooded her thinking, and it was like she couldn't "turn them off." She had no peace. And what was worse, she didn't have answers to any of her questions. She was filled with rage over James's absolute selfishness. *"Doesn't he care?" "How could a man leave his whole family like this?"* How was Lisa to process this tragedy?

Being a Christian, Lisa wondered where God was in all this and wrestled with more questions: "Doesn't God care about us?" "Why wouldn't he protect us from this?" "Why did he let this happen?" Lisa's parents and friends tried to console her by telling her that God is in control and reminding her of Matthew 6:34, "Therefore do not be anxious about tomorrow, for tomorrow will be anxious for itself," and Philippians 4:6, "Do not be anxious about anything," but this wasn't helping. How could she understand this tragedy in light of an all-powerful, all-present, and all-loving God?

Understanding Anxiety

Anxiety is another name for fear, or worry. In this book, I'll use them interchangeably. Anxiety is the most common mental illness in the US, affecting 40 million adults every year.[8] Anxiety can be described as an intense feeling of discomfort, uneasiness, or distress about a current or future threat, that interferes with daily function. It can cause cognitive and physical symptoms, like restlessness, irritability, fatigue, difficulty concentrating, muscle tension, and difficulties with sleep.

When anxiety includes panic, the following symptoms can be present:

- Rapid or pounding heart

- Sweating

- Trembling or shaking

- Shortness of breath

- Feelings of choking

- Chest pain or discomfort

- Nausea or stomach pain

- Feeling dizzy, unsteady, or lightheaded

- Feeling hot or cold

- Numbness or tingling sensations

- Feeling that things are not real or that you are not really a part of yourself (like you are watching yourself)

- Fear of losing control or "going crazy"

- Fear of dying[9]

This is an awful experience, and it can be debilitating. It can significantly affect your work productivity and relationships. Over 70 percent of people who attempt suicide have an active anxiety disorder at the time of the attempt.[10] Anxiety can also negatively affect your nervous, cardiovascular, digestive, immune, and respiratory systems.[11]

Anxiety is a common experience during and following tragedy. Depending on the tragic situation, we could experience worry or fear that the situation will continue, get worse, happen again, or have life-altering consequences to us or our loved ones. This worry or fear can lead to any of the physical or mental symptoms mentioned. Anxiety is a feeling, or emotion. The words *feeling* and *emotion* are used interchangeably. Anxiety is an emotion, like being happy, sad, or lonely are emotions. It's a feeling that comes from how we think, because how we think affects how we feel.

Anxiety and Thoughts

Anxiety is a feeling that follows the thought that we are in real or perceived danger. This is normal, healthy, and adaptive when there is a real threat. When a threat is present, a tiny almond-shaped structure in our brain, called the amygdala, activates to release hormones like cortisol, adrenaline, and noradrenaline in our body, so that we can protect ourselves and those around us. These hormones prepare our bodies for a fight or flight response. For example, if I'm hiking and see a coiled rattlesnake, fear is the appropriate response. As hormones surge through my body, I'm prompted to steer clear or walk away from it. If it attacks me, I can fight back. Taking appropriate precautions when hiking, driving, or preparing for an exam, or making healthy lifestyle changes following a life-threatening diagnosis are all examples of anxiety working well and doing its job. Anxiety working in this way is healthy and adaptive, a gift from God to keep us alive.

Anxiety that is prolonged, extreme, or in response to a threat that is not real or is not imminent can be unhealthy and maladaptive. Rather than just taking precautions, deciding to never go hiking anywhere ever again after seeing a rattlesnake on a hike is an example of anxiety that is unhealthy and maladaptive. Consider also the following examples of anxiety that are unhealthy and maladaptive:

- Worry or fear about an illness or accident that has not occurred and is not likely to occur.

- Worry about a child or loved one getting injured or lost when there is no reason for this.

- Fear over losing one's job or a spouse walking out when there is no evidence that it might happen.

- Prolonged or extreme anxiety that lasts months or years after a tragedy has occurred or a threat has passed.

- Obsessive thinking and preparing for situations to the detriment of other responsibilities.

There is also a kind of anxiety I wanted to mention that's *just there*. There has been no tragedy, it's just that the person runs anxious. Their mind and body are always in fight or flight. My anxiety usually comes after something bad has happened, or when I am afraid that something bad is going to happen. But I've worked with plenty of people who are anxious all the time, and it's not necessarily tied to anything specific. If this is where you find yourself, I do want to encourage you to think deeply about your anxiety and see if there are actually worrisome thoughts about something specific. Often when people say, "I'm just anxious for no reason," there can be a reason that is not easily detected. Not always, but it is good to do some metathinking (thinking about your thoughts), to see if there is anything in your life or your thinking that is making you anxious. Again, there may not be. You may have a steady-state, chronic anxiety that's kind of the white noise in the background of your life all the time.

I also want to mention and acknowledge that anxiety can be present that is not necessarily related to a tragedy. In these cases, it's almost like the anxiety itself is the tragedy. Anxiety is the problem that has occurred in your life that is producing more anxiety, or even other feelings like depression or anger. Or it could be that you have experienced tragedy in your life that has not been fully dealt with, so your anxiety is more remotely caused by the prior tragedies, rather than directly and immediately. Whatever shape anxiety takes in your life, stay with me through this book as we unpack the various ways to think about our anxieties, tragedies, and sufferings that will hopefully alleviate all or much of the anxiety you are feeling.

Anxiety in the Bible

Now that we have briefly discussed what anxiety is, clinically and practically, I want to move on to discussing God's perspective on anxiety as presented in the Bible. For Christians, it's important to have a biblical worldview of our emotions, since emotions make up a big part of who we are. If anxiety is something you have ever struggled with, it's a good idea to search God's word on this matter. Unlike many health-related issues we can face in life (e.g., cancer, diabetes, high blood pressure, etc.), which the Bible does not specifically mention, the Bible does talk specifically about anxiety. This is important for Christians because, as with other matters, there are certain cultural views that have been created to understand anxiety; some are helpful, and some are not. We should always check our cultural beliefs against God's word when the Bible speaks on a topic. Since the Bible speaks on anxiety, let's listen.

As we move through this chapter, remember the definition of anxiety. Anxiety is another name for fear or worry and can be described as an intense feeling of discomfort, uneasiness, or distress about a current or future threat, that interferes with daily function. I take the position that there is a certain kind of anxiety that Christians, who are walking in the Spirit, should *not* feel. I'll explain the different kinds of anxiety later in this chapter. For now, consider the following verses:

> There is no fear in love, but perfect love casts out fear. For fear has to do with punishment, and whoever fears has not been perfected in love. (1 John 4:18)

> God gave us a spirit not of fear but of power and love and self-control. (2 Timothy 1:7)

> Do not be anxious about anything, but in everything by prayer and supplication with thanksgiving let your requests be made known to God. (Philippians 4:6)

These statements are fairly clear. There is a certain type of fear, or anxiety, that should not take residence in the mind of a believer. However, over and over in the Bible, God's people are afraid. It is probably the most common negative emotion experienced by God's people throughout the Bible. And the godliest of people in the Bible experienced it: Abraham, Moses, Joshua, Gideon, David, Elijah, Nehemiah, Isaiah, Jeremiah, Ezekiel, and all the apostles, including Peter and Paul. This is quite a roster. If there were ever a spiritual MVP list, this would be it, and they all experienced anxiety at some point in their lives. David even expected it and said to God, "*When* I am afraid, I put my trust in you" (Psalm 56:3, emphasis mine). God, knowing their internal struggles, does not let them sit in their anxiety endlessly. He acknowledges their fear and either directly tells them not to be afraid or gives them reasons not to fear. Let's discuss three of the people on our MVP list.

Abraham

Abraham feared a foreign king on two separate occasions, and thinking that the king would kill him for his beautiful wife, Sarah, he lied to each king, telling them that Sarah was his sister, not his wife (Genesis 12:10–20 and all of Genesis 20). God not only protected Abraham from harm on each occasion, but prevented the kings from committing sin against him and Sarah, and protected Sarah from becoming the wife of either of these kings. But perhaps the greatest fear Abraham had was in not fathering children. During this fear, God came to him in a vision and said to him, "Fear not, Abram, I am your shield; your reward shall be very great" (Genesis 15:1–2).

Moses

In Exodus 3 and 4, Moses was afraid to speak to Pharoah. Three times Moses complained to God, making excuses for why he couldn't speak to Pharoah as God commanded. In Exodus 3:11, Moses says to God, "Who am I that I should go to Pharaoh and bring the children of Israel out of Egypt?" In other words, "I'm no one. Why would Pharoah listen to me?" God answers by saying to Moses, "I will be with you" (Exodus 3:12). In other words, "You're right, Moses, you are no one. But that doesn't matter. I will be with you."

Then Moses complained that the Egyptians wouldn't believe that God was with him. So God shows Moses two miraculous signs and explains that miracles will be done in Egypt. Then Moses complained that he was not eloquent in speech. God's answer? "Who has made man's mouth? Who makes him mute, or deaf, or seeing, or blind? Is it not I, the Lord? Now therefore go, and I will be with your mouth and teach you what you shall speak" (Exodus 4:11–12). Unfortunately, Moses ended up telling God to send someone else.

Gideon

When God called Gideon to conquer the Israelites' oppressors, the Midianites, Gideon was hiding in a winepress. The angel of the Lord called him a "mighty man of valor" (Judges 6:12). Yet Gideon was afraid, stating that he was the weakest man in his family. And after God said that he, God, would be with him, Gideon asked for a visible sign to confirm it was God speaking to him. Gideon was indeed a "mighty man of valor," but he struggled for courage the entire time. Twice in the narrative, Gideon asked for a sign (Judges 6:17, 36–37). Why? Because he was afraid, and the signs gave him courage. God did not rebuke Gideon for these requests; rather, he gave Gideon what he requested each time. God knew what Gideon needed and even gave him a sign when he didn't ask for it (Judges 7:9–15).

For someone who struggles with anxiety, this is very encouraging: I'm not alone; people of great faith have struggled with this powerful emotion. Certainly, God knows and understands the brain's tendency to fear, for he created it. God put that tiny almond-shaped structure, the amygdala, in our brains that is responsible for our anxiety. When I'm scared, he gets it, is compassionate, and is reassuring. He provides ample verses in the Bible for us to lean on when we are scared. But just as there is appropriate anxiety in normal life situations, like the example I gave about the rattlesnake, so there is appropriate anxiety when it comes to our faith.

Appropriate Biblical Anxiety

There are some examples in the Bible of fear, or anxiety, that are appropriate and right, and that I have no intention of trying to eliminate. Certainly, if you are not walking with God or have committed a sin, there may be appropriate reasons to be anxious. Jacob was appropriately anxious when meeting his brother Esau after Jacob had deceived their father Isaac and stolen Esau's inheritance (Genesis 32:6–7a). This is *not* the kind of anxiety I aim to get rid of.

King Belshazzar was appropriately anxious after sinning against God by drinking out of the vessels of gold and silver that were removed from the temple in Jerusalem. After the famous writing-on-the-wall incident occurred as a proclamation of God's judgment on him, it says, "Then the king's color changed, and his thoughts alarmed him; his limbs gave way, and his knees knocked together" (Daniel 5:6). His anxiety was appropriate, and this is *not* the kind of anxiety I aim to get rid of.

Or consider Ananias and Sapphira. After separately lying to the Apostle Peter regarding money from the sale of a house, they both died. When the church found out about this, it says, "Great fear came upon the whole church and upon all who heard of these things" (Acts 5:11). Of course they were afraid. And this fear was healthy and appropriate. This also is *not* the kind of anxiety I aim to get rid of.

Additionally, the Bible is filled with passages about having an appropriate fear of God. This means to have a right perspective of God, standing in awe of his power and greatness, and giving him ultimate respect and admiration. See Deuteronomy 6:1–2, 1 Samuel 12:14, 2 Kings 17:39, Job 28:28, Psalm 19:9, Proverbs 1:7, 2 Corinthians 5:11, and 1 Peter 2:17. To tremble with amazement and awe at the splendor and power of our almighty God is totally appropriate. We should have an appropriate fear before an all-powerful, all-knowing, ever-present, sovereign God. Paul had a type of anxiety, or intense concern, for the churches, which was also appropriate (2 Corinthians 11:28). These are not the kinds of fears that I am attempting to get rid of.

Before I became a Christian at age twenty, I lived a life full of sin, as I described in the introduction. I wasn't even trying to do good. Quite the contrary. Certain sins were enjoyable to me, and I searched them out. When I came to realize the great offenses I was making toward a perfectly holy and all-powerful God, I was afraid. When I realized that my sin put Jesus on the cross and saw the reality of God in this world, I was like the Philippian jailer in Acts 16, who "trembling with fear he fell down before Paul and Silas" and then asked the only sensible question anyone in his, or my, condition could ask: "Sirs, what must I do to be saved?" (Acts 16:30). This anxiety was used by God and was absolutely necessary to bring me to repentance and into the arms of Jesus.

It has happened since I became a Christian as well. When I have fallen into old habits of sin, *anxiety* is the word I would use to describe my feelings as I thought about the potential consequences of my sin. This is good. After receiving such good favor from God, I was ungrateful and threw his grace back at him. This bothered me. And thank God it did! Paul, in Romans 1, talks about a people with dead consciences, saying that God "gave them up to a debased mind to do what ought not to be done" (v. 28). This is when sin no longer bothers you. It's scary to think about, but that's the alternative to this kind of anxiety. Having feelings of distress following sin to move you to repentance is better than not caring. I would prefer not to sin at all, but if willful, deliberate sin happens, I'm glad that I am alarmed.

So, if this is not the kind of anxiety I am trying to get rid of, what kind of anxiety should we be focused on eliminating?

The Anxiety to Conquer

The kind of anxiety (fear, worry) I aim to conquer is the anxiety in a Christian who is walking in the Spirit while trying to be righteous and obedient to God, when their life is shattered by some tragedy, and as a result, they experience anxiety. I also want the Christian who has not experienced a certain tragedy, but fears that it will happen for one reason or another, to conquer their anxiety. This is the Christian who worries that something bad will happen, that the rug will be pulled out from under them and their life will collapse. When we experience anxiety of this type, I think there is good reason in Scripture for us not to fear. This is the kind of anxiety I wish to eradicate. The kind of anxiety that God (Isaiah 35:3–4), Jesus (Matthew 6:25–34), and the Apostle Paul (Philippians 4:6–7) said to avoid.

As an aside, I want to acknowledge that there is a kind of anxiety that may have started with a cognitive worry, but has developed into something wholly physical, like recurrent panic, or the fight-or-flight response remaining active all the time when there is no real threat. This is when anxiety is no longer just about how you are thinking and is more about what is happening in your body. The fight-or-flight response has been triggered, and it's not turning off. The chemicals involved in anxiety that I mentioned above (e.g., cortisol, adrenaline, and noradrenaline) are constantly active in your body producing what can seem like an unfixable problem that no cognitive change will affect. Much of what I say in this chapter, and much of what this book covers, may not help with this kind of anxiety. Just like cognitive change will not heal your cancer, diabetes, or heart disease, it may not heal this kind of anxiety. Medical intervention, sleep, dietary changes, and other therapeutic interventions to calm the fight-or-flight response may be what is needed. So please keep in mind that the anxiety that I discuss in this chapter, and the anxiety that is helped by cognitive change, is anxiety that is primarily in the mind (e.g., worry), and secondarily in the body, not vice versa.

Coming back to the type of anxiety that cognitive change *will* affect, I don't think that God, which includes Jesus, can experience anxiety in this sense. We will talk more about what he does feel in the next two chapters, but to clarify briefly now, God can have a type of sadness (different from ours) but does not get depressed, and his anger is not the sinful kind. Again, anxiety has been described as an intense feeling of discomfort, uneasiness, or distress about a current or future threat, that interferes with daily function. God, who "is over all and through all and in all" (Ephesians 4:6) and declares "the end from the beginning" (Isaiah 46:10) does not ever feel threatened, and his daily function is never compromised.

The anxiety described in this chapter is anxiety that every human feels at times and that can be conquered when we learn to think differently. I take the position that anxiety, as it has been described here, should have no presence in the Christian's life. Thinking rightly about the God of the Bible eradicates anxiety in our life. I use words like *conquer, eradicate, eliminate,* and *get rid of* on purpose. I do mean to use these words because I believe that as Christians, we can expect this outcome. These words carry the meaning of how the Bible describes what should happen to our anxieties.

I don't use words like *manage, improve,* or *reduce* to describe what should happen to our anxieties, because those words carry meanings about anxiety not found in the Bible. That doesn't mean that our anxieties are not *managed, improved,* or *reduced,* it just means that to talk about them with only these words misses the mark on what God would like us to do with them, and what he says is possible. He wants us to conquer, eradicate, eliminate, and get rid of them. He wants us to utterly destroy our anxiety.

Jesus (Matthew 6:25) and Paul (Philippians 4:6) commanded us to not be anxious. How should we take this? Well, how should we take other commands in the Bible to not be or do something?

> Do not judge. (Matthew 7:1)
> Do not lie. (Colossians 3:9)
> Do not commit adultery. (James 2:11)
> Do not be unequally yoked with unbelievers. (2 Corinthians 6:14)
> Do not be idolators. (1 Corinthians 10:7)
> Do not be conformed to this world. (Romans 12:2)

The Bible says, "Do not be anxious" because God really believes this is possible. What if we said, "I'm just going to *manage* my deceitfulness." Or "I'm going to *reduce* my adultery." We'd say that falls short of God's desire for our life and misses the mark on how he would want us to handle something that is hurting us and those around us.

Anxiety is something that starts in the mind, so we are asked to change our way of thinking. We are asked not to think in a way that leads to anxiety, as happens when we elevate our circumstances and reduce God to a humanistic level. Someone once said that worry is to elevate the natural and strangle the divine. How true. When we think our situation is outside God's control, governance, or plan, we have reduced God to someone who is fallible; someone more like us. Then we have elevated our situation to idolatrous levels. Anything that is bigger than God in our mind has the potential to be an idol. It becomes stronger and more powerful than God, so that we would make *God* bow to *it*. We may not think about it exactly like that in our minds, but when God becomes weaker than that thing, we have made a golden calf of our situation.

If a tragedy has not happened, and we worry that it will, we play the constant "what if" game. "What if such and such happens? If it does, I won't be able to handle it. My life will be ruined. I won't be able to move on. God could not come through or bring good into that situation." So we don't trust that God's plan may *include* tragedy. And we don't trust that if God's plan includes tragedy, then it's for our good, and he is in complete and total control of all the variables involved in a situation to bring about his perfect will. Ultimately, we don't trust that he is going to take care of us *even if* such and such happens. Rather than living with a mindset of "even if" followed by a solid, unequivocal period, we're stuck in the "what if" followed by a vague, ambiguous question mark.

Let's say my son is anxious about whether we are going to have enough to eat for dinner tonight, and I tell him not to worry. If he continues to worry, that shows me that he really doesn't trust that I am able to provide for him. If I have a history of not providing enough food for the family, then his lack of trust in me is warranted. But if he has always had plenty to eat, then his mistrust in me is probably unwarranted, and I'd have to dig deeper to figure out what the issue is. God is not at all like me. He never fails, falls short, or makes mistakes. He has never given us a reason to worry. Anxiety, the type that can be eradicated by a change in thinking, really is an absence of trust in the all-powerful, all-wise, sovereign God who said he will provide for all our needs (Philippians 4:19).

God really believes we can obtain mastery over our thoughts (2 Corinthians 10:5; Philippians 4:8). Just like he expects us to not have lustful thoughts, so we should not have anxious thoughts. And just like we should attack our thoughts of lust, hatred, jealousy, bitterness, and self-pity, we should also attack our anxious thoughts. When we are tempted to be anxious, we are really being tempted not to trust God. Don't let this unbelief sit in your mind. Put it to death.

Now, just like lustful thoughts, killing anxiety is not a one-and-done action. It's not like if you kill lust one day, you are never going to lust again for the rest of your life, though that should be your goal and expectation. You may need to kill your lust, hatred, self-pity, or anxiety every single day. If you are prone to being anxious, this is a battle you will continue to fight. To conquer anxiety does not mean that you kill it once and it never comes back to life. You keep killing it over and over again. That's how we need to look at the problem of anxiety.

And this is our goal: that knowing the God of the Bible will produce such an enormous trust in him that anxiety will not have any room left in our mind, and that this will result in peace. Anxiety starts in our mind, so any intervention aimed at resolving our anxiety must address how we think. Rethinking our thoughts, emotions, tragedy, and sufferings will help us on this path.

Finding Peace

Finding peace in the face of tragedy is not easy. How we think during and following tragedy will make a difference in how we feel. I have labored in these pages to show that God cares deeply about our thought life, since how we think affects how we feel and live. The goal of this book is to help us think differently in times of tragedy, resulting in less anxiety and more peace.

You will find that each chapter in this section, "Finding Peace in Our Feelings," does *not* have a section with interventions to address each emotion (i.e., anxiety, depression, and anger). This is because this entire book is an intervention toward our thoughts in order to address each feeling. Every chapter is a call toward thinking differently about our lives in light of horrific tragedy that has come or will come. And this is not easy. There is not a three-step process or a quick and easy fix to thinking differently. Cognitive change requires effort. Like turning a ship, sometimes cognitive change takes a while. But be patient with yourself. You've been thinking a certain way for a long time, and it takes time to change. Read each chapter, more than once if you have to, to get a grasp on the way God wants you to see tragedy, suffering, and your life in light of your present reality. Let's continue forward as we explore the remaining two feelings, depression and anger.

Journal Questions

1. This chapter started with Lisa's story. Putting yourself in Lisa's shoes, can you relate to her struggle to understand God in light of her tragedy? While you may not have experienced what she did, you may have experienced tragedy of this magnitude or greater. When tragedy strikes, what questions do you ask? Is it ok to process tragedy by asking God questions? Journaling is a process of reflection and discovery. If it feels right to you, write down a list of questions you have for God about the tragedy you are experiencing. While you may not receive an answer, expressing your questions to God in writing is a healthy step in processing your pain.

2. What do you think about how Lisa was thinking and the questions she asked about God? Not now, but eventually, if her questions and thoughts about God persist like this, is there anything you could say, or ask, that might help her through this? As Lisa processes what happened to her and her children, is there a way that she could start to think about this tragedy that will help her?

3. How does it feel to know that the great MVPs of the Bible struggled with anxiety? Think about the biblical figures mentioned in this chapter. Can you relate to any of them? How did God help them through their anxiety? Is God helping you in similar ways?

4. I talked about conquering anxiety and not just managing it. What are some ways that we tend to manage our anxiety? What would it look like to conquer yours? What would your life look like if you were to put anxiety to death?

5. What are some anxious thoughts that you are having? How does God want you think about each of these?

CHAPTER 5

Depression

Jennifer is a twenty-six-year-old newly married woman with no children. She married her high school sweetheart, Ryan, about six months ago. Jennifer is a college graduate and works full time in accounting. Her husband completed a college degree and is in his third year of medical school to become a family physician.

Ryan is a loving husband and hardworking man. Despite his busy schedule, he makes time every week to take Jennifer on a date. They love getting sushi together and talking about their week. Ryan is passionate about medicine and helping people, and can't wait to be a fully practicing doctor. Jennifer loves hearing Ryan's passion and is inspired by him. Ryan is a faithful Christian, and often talks about his calling to help people as a medical missionary in developing countries while spreading the gospel. Jennifer beams whenever Ryan talks about this, and she looks forward to their many adventures together.

They often talk about children, buying a home, and what their neighborhood will look like. Jennifer and Ryan grew up in stable, Christian homes, with each of their parents still together. They have a great relationship with their parents and often go to their houses for meals. The talk eventually turns toward children and when Ryan and Jennifer will be giving their parents grandchildren. Ryan and Jennifer both came from big families. Ryan was a middle child, and Jennifer was the youngest. Family get-togethers were large gatherings, with lots of families with kids. Ryan and Jennifer have great footsteps to follow in as they plan out their lives.

As Jennifer thought about her life, she was incredibly grateful to God for how much he had blessed her. She was grateful to have grown up in a Christian home with loving, stable parents who taught her about the preciousness of God and relationships. Ryan was Jennifer's first and only intimate relationship, and they waited until marriage for intimacy. Jennifer grew up in church but saw many of her friends jumping in an out of relationships and being boy crazy. She saw things differently and felt that God wanted her to focus more on her relationship with him and serving others, instead of chasing guys around. During high school and college, she was devoted to her youth and college ministries, serving others, and sharing her faith on her campuses. Thankfully, during that time, God blessed her with Ryan, and the two were a perfect match. They got married right out of college and became involved in the young married ministry in their church.

One day, Ryan began having severe migraines and dizziness. Ryan and Jennifer thought it was due to stress, as third-year medical students have a lot on their plates. The frequency of these symptoms began to increase, and Ryan started having vision changes and trouble concentrating. All this was totally out of the norm for Ryan. In high school, he was an AP honors graduate and captain of the wrestling team. In college he maintained a 4.0 GPA. Something was very wrong, and Jennifer was stricken with worry.

Ryan was scheduled to see his doctor the next day when he collapsed while walking from Jennifer's car to the front door. He was rushed to the hospital and received an MRI. The oncologist was called in, and Ryan was diagnosed with stage four brain cancer. The cancer had metastasized, making surgery unfeasible. The oncologist gave radiation little hope and said that Ryan and his family should make preparations for his death, which could be in as little as a few months. What?! No one could believe it. Ryan? There's no way. There must be some mistake. Ryan, Jennifer, their families, and their church began to pray diligently. Many of them fasted and prayed. Ryan continued to deteriorate. Three months later, he was dead.

How could anyone make sense of this? It didn't make sense. Everyone, especially Jennifer, was in complete shock and disbelief. Jennifer was experiencing what is called *derealization*, which means that the situation and everything around her seemed unreal, like she was living in a dream, or more like a nightmare. She experienced a range of emotions, including anxiety, depression, and anger, emotions she had never felt before. But the most prominent was depression. She had never experienced anything like this.

Jennifer wasn't sleeping, and she barely ate. She didn't want to socialize or leave the house. Visitors were welcome, but she retreated to her room while they were there. Normal activities seemed impossible to complete. She moved very slowly through tasks, and it seemed that everything around her was moving slowly too. She used to go nonstop, and now she could barely get out of bed. She found little comfort in things that used to make her happy. Life was different.

Jennifer's thoughts were troubling. She first thought about Ryan. How could this happen to him? He was the perfect guy: a model student and athlete with dreams to serve God as a medical missionary, who married a Christian woman in his early twenties instead of running around sleeping with different women like most of his college buddies. Now dead at twenty-four from brain cancer?

Then she thought about her own life. How did it go from nearly perfect to this? She did everything right; she followed the rules. She lived her whole life in devotion to Jesus, went to church weekly, prayed and read her Bible daily, and served others regularly. God took away her husband before they could really get started on life together. It hit her that she would live the rest of her life and never see his face, never hear his voice, and never feel his touch again. She would never have children with him. Never have any more dates or adventures together. She wanted to die to be with him.

She thought about how unfair it is that men who treat God with contempt and neglect their families seem to thrive, while her poor husband suffered miserably with this disease that took his life at such a young age. Regret and guilt tormented her. How did she miss this? How could this have happened? Were there signs she should have noticed that would have led her to seek help from doctors sooner? And did she give him the life he deserved? Was she the best wife she could be for the time he had? Most of all, she missed Ryan deeply. It was a depth of sadness that she didn't know was possible. And where was God in all this? How could he let this happen? Was he too weak, or busy, or uncaring? Or maybe he doesn't even exist. That possibility scared her. How in the world was Jennifer to make any sense of this tragedy?

Understanding Depression

Depression is the leading cause of disability in the US.[12] Nearly 17.3 million US adults suffer with a depressive disorder.[13] Depression can be described as feeling sad, empty, hopeless, and irritable, and results in a loss of interest or pleasure in activities. It also can include excessive weight loss or weight gain, insomnia (difficulty falling or staying asleep) or hypersomnia (excessive sleepiness), restlessness, fatigue, feelings of worthlessness, difficulty concentrating, and thoughts of death and suicide.[14] Depression can affect nearly every aspect of your life, including your relationships, productivity, and academic and occupational functioning. It can also lead to substance abuse and serious health consequences.[15]

Think about that number: over 17 million North American adults. That's a lot of people. The state of New York has a population of about 19 million. That means there are enough depressed people in this country to make up an entire state. And depression not only affects the individual, but the entire network of individuals with whom the depressed person is close. Let's say everyone knows at least four people well. That would mean 68 million people are affected by depression. That would be more than twice the population of Texas!

Like anxiety, depression is a feeling, or an emotion. It's something you feel in response to how you are thinking. As with other feelings, it's not the situation that depresses us, but it's how we think about the situation that depresses us. This is not to say that depression is avoidable during a horrible, life-altering circumstance, like the one described above. But it is to say that how we think during that horrible, life-altering circumstance will make a huge difference in how we feel. I have worked with people in the aftermath of the most horrific events who are not depressed. And I have worked with people after events of less magnitude who are severely depressed. The main difference between the two groups is how they process or think about the event. It's not the situation that determines your mood, but the way you think about it. For a catastrophically lighter situation than what has been described above, consider the following examples.

Eric and Gina

Eric came to me depressed after getting laid off from his dream job. Eric was in his early thirties, married, with two children. He and his wife both worked. Eric's thoughts centered around not being able to provide for his family, his inability to find a new job in a tough market, his limited skillset, and being the "husband who is supported by his wife." Despite a six-month severance package, Eric said things like, "I'll never be able to make what I was making there," "No one's going to hire me," and "I feel like a loser."

Gina, on the other hand, presented for therapy with a very similar situation. She was also in her early thirties and was the single mom of a young child. Gina was laid off from her dream job, which she had had since graduating from college almost ten years prior, and was also given a six-month severance package. Gina wanted help processing her situation and wanted some direction in moving into a new career field. She was not depressed. It was noticed that she had a lot of peace and was generally happy. She talked about the new opportunities that could open up for her, the fact that she had six months to figure something out, that through this she could teach her daughter a lesson on perseverance during hardship, and that she had skills that would be valuable to an employer.

What is the difference between Eric and Gina? Both were laid off from their dream job. On the surface, Gina's situation actually seemed more problematic than Eric's, in that she was a single mom with a young daughter, and Eric had a spouse with a job. Yet Eric was depressed, while Gina was not. What was it that made one person feel awful and the other person feel happy and peaceful? The difference was in how they *thought*. You may say that losing a job is one thing, but losing a child to cancer is another. And you may say that it's easier to avoid becoming depressed over a lesser tragedy, and that one is more likely to become depressed over a greater tragedy. You may be right. But regardless of the magnitude of the tragedy, how you think during that tragedy will impact the length and severity of your depression.

Depression vs. Sadness

We should at this point distinguish between depression and sadness. Sadness is not depression, though if you are depressed, you may be sad.

Depression was defined above, in the first paragraph under the heading "Understanding Depression." Sadness is a normal part of life and will normally be experienced during and following a tragedy. This is healthy. Even severe sadness can be normal and is not depression. Depression is a specific feeling, accompanied by the other symptoms mentioned in this section. The definition I used for *depression* above is a medical one, from *DSM-5-TR*.[16] This is the best definition of depression I know of, and it is the one I use in my practice to understand what I see in the patients who come to my office.

When I use the word *depression* and describe it in this way, I don't at all mean that you should not feel depressed over your situation. Your feeling of depression may be perfectly valid and appropriate, though most people do not like feeling this way. They want to work through their depression and get back to their life. They are weighed down by the feelings of guilt, shame, regret, worthlessness, and hopelessness, and find it hard to complete normal, everyday tasks. *Depression* only defines what a person is feeling. It does not label it as right or wrong.

In distinguishing sadness from depression, understand that the ability to feel sad is God-given. It is part of having a sensitive heart to the cold realities of this world. I want to feel sad over the horrible suffering and wretched evils around me, and I want to be around people who are sensitive in this way. A sensitive, godly sadness (sorrow) over the suffering and lostness of this world is part of being made in God's image. May we never become numb to the harsh realities of this world. However, to go from sadness to depression, and to stay relentlessly in depression day in and day out, is not honoring God or bearing his image. In fact, it is more like an abandonment of godly thinking. It's a full embrace of helplessness and hopelessness that is the opposite of a godly response to the horrors of this world.

"Just There" Depression

Often, depression comes in response to how we are thinking about and processing a specific tragedy in our life. Or, like anxiety, depression can stem from more remote tragedies that a person has experienced in their life and has not yet fully dealt with. However, sometimes depression occurs for no identifiable reason at all. It's not rooted in any specific tragedy or in how the person is thinking about a tragedy. It's just *there*. In these cases, it's almost like the depression *is* the tragedy the person is dealing with. And we know from the description of symptoms already mentioned that it can be debilitating.

I think this is the kind of depression my dad had when I was growing up. On the outside, it looked like he had the perfect life: a good job, money, a house, his health, a wife, and kids. He had a tough upbringing, which I think contributed to his depression, but there were no real tragedies, at least not that I knew about, that we could say were responsible for his depression. Yet he was severely depressed my whole life. And this depression was debilitating. He had a hard time going to work or helping around the house. I remember endless hours of him watching television, or in my later years, being in front of a computer. He didn't socialize with friends or talk to us. He was angry much of the time. His depression affected virtually every aspect of his life and ours.

I mention this type of depression to acknowledge that not all depression is tied to specific thinking about a tragedy, and that depression itself can be the tragedy. Either way, as with my dad, we can have depressive thoughts of hopelessness, helplessness, and worthlessness that tear us apart, making our depression worse and creating what seems like an endless cycle of depression. So, whether you find yourself depressed over a specific tragedy, or depression itself is the tragedy, stay with me as we consider depression from a biblical perspective.

Sadness and Depression in the Bible

I think there are people in the Bible who were depressed, even by the medical definition I've used in this chapter. This doesn't mean that all sad people in the Bible were depressed, but it seems like at least some were. As I mentioned above, depression is different from sadness, even deep sadness. Sadness is a feeling we get when we experience certain situations that hurt us or others. It is an appropriate response when we or others experience tragedy, loss, and suffering. Godly men and women felt sadness, and even God himself felt a type of sadness.

Genesis 6:5–6 comes close to a description of sadness experienced by God when he saw the wickedness of men on the earth. "The Lord saw that the wickedness of man was great in the earth, and that every intention of the thoughts of his heart was only evil continually. And the Lord regretted that he had made man on the earth, and it grieved him to his heart."

God regretting and God grieving can be described as a type of sadness. *Regret*, in Hebrew, is the word *naham* and connotes the idea of being sorry, moved to pity, and suffering grief. Picture God in heaven giving a big sigh as he looks down on the people he created. *Grieved*, in Hebrew, is the word *asab* and connotes the idea of an emotional hurt, pain, or displeasure. This is something God felt. God was grieved in his heart as he looked upon the sinfulness of humankind. Put simply, our sin makes God sad.

Listen to God's response to the sin of his people Israel through his prophet Jeremiah:

> My joy is gone; grief is upon me;
> > my heart is sick within me. (8:18)
> For the wound of the daughter of my people is my heart wounded;
> > I mourn, and dismay has taken hold on me. (8:21)
> Oh that my head were waters,
> > and my eyes a fountain of tears
> that I might weep day and night
> > for the slain of the daughter of my people! (9:1)

Jesus also experienced a type of sadness. Isaiah 53:3 describes Jesus as "a man of sorrows and acquainted with grief." John 11:35 tells us that Jesus wept when his friend Lazarus died. Luke 19:41 says that Jesus wept over Jerusalem when he considered their present spiritual condition and their future destruction.

Emotion, in this case the emotion of sadness, is an emotion experienced by God, and Jesus, our creator. Being created in the image of God (Genesis 1:26–27), we share this capacity to feel sadness. As has been mentioned, this is a good thing because a person's experience of sadness shows their heart is sensitive, especially when it is expressed in sympathy toward the weaknesses, losses, and sufferings of others. The unfeeling, unmoved, unsympathetic person is not acting in God's image or being like Jesus, and is not the model we should imitate.

David

Throughout the Bible, God's people have been moved to sadness at appropriate times. King David is an example of this. David was called a man after God's own heart (1 Samuel 13:14). At least seven times in the narrative of David's life we are told that he wept.

- David wept with Jonathan when he had to flee Jerusalem from King Saul (1 Samuel 20:41)

- David and his men wept when they found out that their wives and sons and daughters were taken captive by the Amalekites at Ziklag (1 Samuel 30:4)

- David wept when King Saul and Jonathan died (2 Samuel 1:12)

- David wept when the son Bathsheba bore to him was sick (2 Samuel 12:22)

- David wept when his son Absalom killed his other son, Amnon (2 Samuel 13:36)

- David wept when he fled Jerusalem from Absalom (2 Samuel 15:30)

- David wept when Absalom died (2 Samuel 18:33)

Various Examples

Some other examples of sadness in the Bible are as follows:

- Hagar when she realized she couldn't provide for the physical needs of her son (Genesis 21:16)

- Abraham when his wife died (Genesis 23:2)

- The Israelites when Moses died (Deuteronomy 34:8)

- Ezra and the Israelites over their sin (Ezra 10:1)

- Nehemiah when he learned the state of Jerusalem (Nehemiah 1:4)

- Hezekiah when he received news he was going to die (Isaiah 38:3)

- The Jews over the destruction plotted against them (Esther 4:3)

- Peter when he denied Jesus (Matthew 26:75)

- "Devout men" when Stephen was stoned to death (Acts 8:2)

- The Apostle Paul and the disciples when Paul was leaving for Jerusalem (Acts 20:37)

- Jeremiah, who has been named the Weeping Prophet because he often lamented over the sin and state of his people, and who even wrote a book in the Bible called Lamentations

God's people were told to express sadness throughout the Bible. God called for weeping and mourning at times (Isaiah 22:12; Joel 2:12). King Solomon and James, the brother of Jesus, call for weeping and mourning at times (Ecclesiastes 3:4; James 4:9). Zechariah predicted that Jerusalem would mourn and weep bitterly over the death of their Messiah, as they should (Zechariah 12:10). The Apostle Paul teaches the Corinthian church that there is such a thing called godly grief, or sorrow, and that this should be experienced by Christians over their sin, as it "produces a repentance that leads to salvation without regret" (2 Corinthians 7:10). And Christians have a paradoxical, simultaneous experience on this earth of being sorrowful, yet always rejoicing (2 Corinthians 6:10).

However, all of this is different from depression. God, including Jesus, was never depressed. Most of the examples listed above were not depression. I can think of at least four people in the Bible who may have actually been depressed, and three of the four were devout men of God: Job, David, Elijah, and King Saul. For the sake of time, I'll briefly discuss two of them.

Job

When it comes to depression, Job is certainly the first person in the Bible to come to mind. He is the figure in the Bible most known for suffering, even by people who don't know the Bible. The Book of Job is about his suffering, which came in different forms, and more specifically, about how he and the other people talked about in the book understood and processed his suffering. Spoiler alert: Job's suffering was not punishment from God for some sin of Job's; rather, it was to demonstrate God's holiness and glory, refine Job's character and holiness, and test Job's faithfulness to God.

The book starts by describing Job as "blameless and upright, one who feared God and turned away from evil" (Job 1:1). Job was married and had ten children. He was very wealthy, so much so that he was described as "the greatest of all the people of the east" (Job 1:3), and was respected in the town square for his wise counsel (Job 29:7, 21–25), his treatment of the poor, the widows, and the blind (Job 29:12–16), and how he dealt with crime (Job 29:17). Yet Job experienced horrific tragedies. Chapters 1 and 2 of the Book of Job present how these tragedies came about. God's hand and plan in these tragedies, along with Satan's involvement and the harm done by the sinful actions of others, is examined in other chapters of this book. For now, we are only considering the effects of these tragedies on Job's mental health. Here's what happened:

- First, the Sabeans killed Job's servants and took his oxen and donkeys.

- Second, "the fire of God fell from heaven," likely lightning, and killed Job's sheep and more of his servants.

- Third, the Chaldeans killed more of Job's servants and took his camels.

- Fourth, a "great wind" came, striking the house where all ten of Job's children were, causing the roof to collapse, which killed all of them.

- Fifth, Job was struck with detestable sores all over his body.

Think about all this. In an instant, Job lost all his children, his wealth, and his health. Even one of these losses is enough to cause someone to be depressed. Job's extensive trauma resulted in what seems like depression. Here are some things he said:

- "Let the day perish on which I was born, and the night that said, 'A man is conceived.'" (3:3)

- "Why did I not die at birth, come out from the womb and expire?" (3:11)

- "Why is light given to him who is in misery, and life to the bitter in soul, who long for death, but it comes not, and dig for it more than for hidden treasures, who rejoice exceedingly and are glad when they find the grave?" (3:20–22)

- "Remember that my life is a breath; my eye will never again see good." (7:7)

- "I loathe my life; I would not live forever. Leave me alone, for my days are a breath." (7:16)

If Job talked this way today to a mental health professional, he'd be on suicide watch. I'm not kidding. Then we see Job wrestling with his thoughts, and his three ignorant and insensitive friends, for the majority of the book. Then God speaks. His answer demonstrates his power and the extensiveness of his involvement in the universe. Ultimately, he restores Job's health and wealth, and gives Job and his wife more children.

Elijah

Elijah is one of the most powerful and well-known prophets in the Old Testament. You may know him for taking on the 450 prophets of Baal on Mount Carmel. After the prophets of Baal called upon their god to answer with fire, and no fire came, Elijah called upon his God, who immediately answered with an enormous blaze from heaven. This amazing display of power resulted in the Israelites worshiping the Lord and siding with the Lord and Elijah. Elijah and the Israelites slaughtered all 450 Baal worshipers that day.

You'll need to read 1 Kings 18:17–40 to get the full picture of this scene. In this account, Elijah is noted for his confidence, courage, and faith, resulting in optimism, leadership, determination, and results as he took on the wicked King Ahab and his prophets. There is nothing here that is even close to what we would consider depression. If Elijah were to tell this story to a friend after it happened, he would be bursting with excitement and unable to sit still as he explained the details of this miraculous event. And it was miraculous. It's hard to believe, then, that a few verses later we find Elijah described in an emotional state that could probably be considered depression.

Queen Jezebel, the wife of King Ahab, swore to kill Elijah by the next day. Apparently, the Queen was more ruthless, and serious, than her husband, because when Elijah heard about it, "he was afraid, and he arose and ran for his life" (1 Kings 19:3). The story picks up in the next verse: "But he himself went a day's journey into the wilderness and came and sat down under a broom tree. And he asked that he might die, saying, 'It is enough; now, O Lord, take away my life, for I am no better than my fathers.' And he lay down and slept under a broom tree" (1 Kings 19:4–5). Elijah had had enough.

One of the greatest indicators of depression is the feeling of hopelessness, the feeling that your situation is never going to be fixed or get better, that you are stuck in this condition forever. And sometimes when a person feels this way, death looks like the better option. This is where Elijah was.

But God answers with compassion, providing Elijah with a good meal and rest (1 Kings 19:6). Then God provides the strength for the prophet to travel forty days and forty nights to Horeb, the mount of God, where God speaks to him through the wind, an earthquake, fire, and a gentle whisper, reminding him of the great God he serves and who is on his side.

It helps to know that depression is not something that only weak and faithless people have. And God's response to these men was not, "Buck up, son. Have more faith!" His intervention was to tell and show them more of himself, to make them realize more of who he is. To help them through their emotional stuck-ness, they needed to see more of God.

Keep Going

As we move through this book, we will see God's continual guidance in helping us think differently about our losses, pain, and suffering. Please know that sadness or depression over tragedy is not wrong and is not to be discouraged. If you have experienced a tragedy in your life, it's ok to feel these things. Sadness is an emotion given to us by God for times like this. Don't feel like you have to rush through it. Let yourself *feel*. But if you find yourself slipping into a depression and getting stuck there, that is not where God wants you to be, and most people want to get out of that feeling. But God is not mad at you for being depressed. However, he may want you to learn to think about him differently through your tragedy and in your depression.

Keep in mind that God is trying to do something with your thinking to help you through your depression. Sometimes, he'll let the thing that has happened stay with you for a while in order to develop or direct your thinking in a certain way. Rather than remove a challenge right away, which is what we want him to do, he may let something linger. God is working on you every day through this, and the thing that has happened has not escaped his attention. He knows exactly what you need in your depression, and he will see you through.

Journal Questions

1. Losing a loved one is one of the most difficult tragedies we can ever experience. This chapter started with the young married couple Jennifer and Ryan. By all accounts, it appeared that they were set up to have a wonderful, God-honoring life and marriage together. But God had other plans. Jennifer was deeply depressed, as was understandable in her situation. If I were to meet Jennifer in that state, I would say that she needs time and space to grieve and process her situation, and that her feelings are valid. I would want her family and friends to be with her during this time and not rush her to feel better. Many tragedies are like this. Sometimes we need time and space to grieve. But these are sometimes hard to find. Too often, we rush back into the busyness of life without allowing ourselves adequate time and space to grieve. If this is where you find yourself, write in your journal how you plan to arrange your life and schedule for this period to take the time and space you need to process what you are feeling.

2. After her husband's death, Jennifer asked where God was in all this, how could he let this happen, was he too weak, or busy, or uncaring, and does he even exist. If Jennifer persists in this way of thinking, and this way of thinking becomes fixed and dominant in her mind, how do you think she will feel? How will her relationship with God be? If this way of thinking goes on, what do you think you could eventually say to her, or ask her, that might help? Is there a way that Jennifer could think about this tragedy that would help her through it?

3. Is there a situation that is depressing you? How can you think about the situation in a way that will help you through your depression? Write down how you are currently thinking about it, and how you can start thinking differently about it.

4. Think about how sadness is not depression, and the biblical examples that were given of each. Do your current feelings relate more to how Jesus and David felt, or how Job and Elijah felt?

5. Reflect on how these mighty men of faith, Job and Elijah, struggled with depression. Does that change how you feel about your depression? How did God help these men with their depression? What did he do? What did he say? Is God helping you through your depression in any of the same ways? Write down whatever ways, even if subtle, God may be trying to help you through your depression.

CHAPTER 6

Anger

Matt is a single father of a seven-year-old girl, Abigail. Matt lived a wild lifestyle in his late teen years and early twenties: in and out of relationships, employment problems, heavy drinking and marijuana use, and dabbling with some harder drugs. He gave his life to Christ in his midtwenties, leaving his promiscuous living, substance use, and instability in his past. Besides seeing his need for Jesus, one other good thing came out of that period in his life: Abigail.

Abigail was born as Matt was in the depths of his prior lifestyle. Abigail's mom was in the same boat as Matt. The two hooked up at a bar for a one-night stand. They exchanged numbers, and she later sent him a text saying she was pregnant.

Abigail's mom didn't want the baby and pushed for an abortion. She wanted Matt's consent, and he almost gave it. Thinking about how to raise a child, when he was still very much a child himself, seemed like an impossible task. But something about abortion seemed wrong. Matt started to clean up his life and committed to a full-time job as an apprentice in the business of heating and air conditioning, with the goal of being on his own some day and starting his own business. Thankfully, Abigail's mom at least minimized her substance use during the pregnancy and committed, though reluctantly, to have the baby.

When Abigail was born, her mom went back to the party life and Matt took care of Abigail while working a full-time job. He wanted a family and even proposed to Abigail's mom. She agreed, but a month later, she was gone. She sent him a long text message about how she just didn't have it in her to raise a child. Matt was on his own to raise Abigail. He struggled for the first couple of years. Going off little sleep, little money, and a lot of caffeine, he made it happen. Miraculously, Abigail made it to preschool in good health and fairly normal development. By this time, Matt was making decent money and had a lot more stability for him and Abigail. He had a great relationship with his daughter, and they began attending church regularly.

Matt's job made it necessary to place Abigail in after-school childcare for a couple of hours a day. It was a childcare service that came to Abigail's preschool to provide care to children of working parents until their parents got off work and picked their children up. One day, Matt noticed that Abigail was acting differently. She was withdrawn, anxious, and irritable. This was different from her normal outgoing, happy self. The behavior concerned him, and he began to inquire about it at Abigail's preschool and after-school care. The teachers and caregivers said they too had noticed the change in Abigail's behavior but were not sure what was the cause. The behavior went on for a couple of weeks.

One day, while Matt was at work, he received a call from the director of Abigail's preschool, who asked Matt to come in immediately. Matt's heart was racing as he rushed to the school. A police car was there. His stomach dropped. With adrenaline pumping through his body, Matt stormed inside and asked what was going on. Abigail was sitting with the director, who asked Matt to sit. Matt did not sit and asked again what was going on. The director said that Abigail was molested by one of the staff of the after-school childcare service. The director said the perpetrator was a new staff member and was caught on video violating Abigail.

Shock, confusion, and rage filled his body. He wanted to kill someone and felt in that moment that he could, though he had never been a violent person in the past. The moments following receiving this news felt like hours. Time moved slower. Everything turned red. As the police officer took down information, Matt demanded answers. How did they let this happen? Don't they do background checks? Where is this person now? How many times did it happen? What exactly happened? How were the police going to find this person? The director's apology and offer to provide Abigail with therapy was not enough. To kill this guy and sue everyone was the only resolution Matt could see.

Thankfully, Matt didn't kill anyone. As he left the school with Abigail, heading to the hospital with the police officer to have Abigail medically evaluated by a physician, and having no idea how to process this with her, Matt was left to his own thoughts. Complete rage filled his mind as he thought about what had happened to his sweet daughter. Anger toward the preschool, the childcare service program, the perpetrator, and God was in the forefront of Matt's mind, and it stayed there. Sometimes the anger was so consuming, Matt felt that he needed something to help him calm down. So he turned to what he knew: substance use. He resumed work, and Abigail resumed school. "You can't stop living," he said, "Besides, I have to pay the bills." But the anger never left him.

The perpetrator was arrested and sentenced. Thankfully, Abigail did not have to testify in court. She had been traumatized enough already. She received therapy to process the abuse, but how in the world was a little girl to process something like this? Matt decided not to pursue a lawsuit against the preschool or childcare service program. He wasn't in the mental space to do this, and it would have dragged this thing out even longer. He decided to let it go, but it did not "let go."

The anger and rage consumed him, with anger at God most prominent. How could God let this happen? Didn't he know? Didn't he care? Or was he unable to stop it? The injustice of it all was baffling. It was so unfair. One sleepless night, Matt said to God, "Didn't I leave everything to follow you? I changed everything, cleaned up my life, made the right choices in the midst of a lot of wrong but tempting options. And you let this happen! If this is the kind of God you are, who lets things like this happen to innocent children, I want no part of you!"

Matt's anger eventually came down to a more functional level. Of course, he was still angry. Any dad would be. But he stopped drinking and using drugs, and the situation no longer consumed him. Abigail turned out ok, processing the situation the best any child could. But they never set foot in a church again, and Matt became an atheist.

Understanding Anger

The American Psychological Association (APA) defines *anger* as "an emotion characterized by antagonism toward someone or something you feel has deliberately done you wrong."[17] Like anxiety and depression, anger is an emotion, or feeling. Anger is something you feel when you perceive that you, or someone you love, has been done wrong. It's that feeling you have when injustice has been done, when things are unfair, when your perception of what's good and right has been disregarded or abused. It's a feeling characterized by antagonism. Other words to describe this feeling are *resentment* and *hostility*. You get the picture, right? Anger is an emotion that everyone has experienced. Anger is a common emotion during and following tragedy.

Anger can be productive and helpful, or destructive and harmful. Productive anger leads to help, while destructive anger leads to harm. Destructive anger is on the rise in the US. Just consider the violent crime statistics over the COVID-19 era.[18],[19],[20] It seems like every week we wake up at least once to news of another mass shooting that has happened somewhere in our country. It appears that around 18 percent of people in North America admit to having a problem with anger.[21] And after watching any social media outlet, any news station, or anything in the political arena, it appears that the other 82 percent are lying!

I think about the wars going on right now as I type. Israel and Palestine, Russia and Ukraine, and the Yemeni civil war, to name a few. The death toll from direct, violent causes and from the indirect effects of war, like famine, displacement, insanitary conditions, and lack of medical care, is staggering. While death tolls are hard to judge, it is estimated that nearly 40,000 people have been killed in the Israeli-Palestinian conflict that started in 2023, nearly 100,000 in the Russia-Ukraine conflict that started in 2022, and nearly 400,000 since the civil war in Yemen started in 2014. That's a lot of dead bodies. And I only mentioned the three major ones that are making most of the headlines. The Geneva Academy is currently monitoring 110 armed conflicts that are occurring throughout the world right now.[22]

It would be difficult to state the many reasons for these conflicts. But we would be remiss to think that anger is not fueling much of the discord between the groups that are currently killing each other. *Hatred* is the word that comes to mind when I think about what drives some of their behaviors.

Killing civilians and hostages, torture, mutilation, and sexual assault are just some of the intentional "war crimes" we've read about this decade.

But military groups are not the only ones angry these days. There are plenty of things right here at home we could be angry about if we let things get to us. And how easily it does get to us. As I write this, some of the current trending topics to get anyone's blood boiling include abortion, climate, COVID, cybersecurity, economy, education, elections, foreign affairs, free speech, gender, guns, immigration, racism, and terrorism. Many people I know have simply chosen to disconnect from news and social media completely, because the things they hear and see trigger too much anger.

Anger, in the immediate sense, is a normal response to an unjust or unfair situation or tragedy, and can be helpful as the body and mind react to the present situation to bring about change. However, chronic, ongoing, and unresolved anger can lead to physical and emotional problems. The long-term physical effects of anger include increased anxiety, depression, high blood pressure, and headache. Long-term anger can also affect your cardiovascular system and increase stroke risk.[23],[24],[25]

Productive Anger

It's been said that anger is the other side of love.[26] What is meant by this is that anger and love go hand in hand. They are not opposites of each other, as the phrase "other side" may imply. They exist together. Without love, you would not feel anger. Our vignette about Matt in this chapter is a perfect example of this. Matt was angry because he loves his daughter. Another way to think about this is that anger is an *expression* of love when injustice has occurred. When someone or something you love has been treated wrongly, unfairly, or sinfully, your love for that someone or something is expressed in your anger toward that treatment.

Anger, as the other side of love, also means that many of the beneficent, or loving, acts and noble purposes toward others originate from anger. Have you ever heard of Mothers Against Drunk Driving (MADD)? MADD is the nation's largest nonprofit organization dedicated to protecting families from drunk driving accidents and underage drinking, with over 600 organizations, chapters, and community action teams across all fifty states and each province of Canada. They partner with some companies you may have heard of: the NFL, Nationwide, Walmart, Farmers Insurance, TikTok, Uber, and Lyft. How did they start? In 1980, one mother experienced the death of her daughter at the hands of a drunk driver. MADD started with anger over a tragedy.

And there are countless organizations and people devoted to helping others through acts of charity, that all originated because someone saw or experienced something that, by our definition of anger, was wrong or unjust and needed correction. Feeding America, Wounded Warrior Project, National Domestic Violence Hotline, American Foundation for Suicide Prevention, the Polaris Project (to fight human trafficking), and Prevent Child Abuse America are all organizations that started with a feeling of anger at some wrong or unjust condition.

Or think about the following people:

- Abraham Lincoln and Harriet Tubman, who fought to end slavery

- Dietrich Bonhoeffer, who fought to end Hitler's extermination of the Jews

- Martin Luther King, Jr., Mahatma Gandhi, and Susan B. Anthony, who fought for human rights and greater equality

- Mother Teresa, who gave her life to help the poor

Angela, a colleague of mine, and her son Corbin are also examples of people who took a horribly tragic situation and directed their anger in a productive way. I first met Angela when my family and I moved to Texas. She was gracious to let me sublease her private practice office to see clients for a few hours a week in the evenings as I was starting my practice here. Shortly after meeting Angela, Corbin was diagnosed with ganglioneuroblastoma, a tumor that arises from nerve tissues, just after his eleventh birthday. The tumor was found by Corbin's pediatrician during a routine physical exam. Corbin had no symptoms. The following is an excerpt taken from https://www.csquadfoundation.org/, by permission from Corbin's mom:

> Six months after removing the tumor, the cancer progressed into its most aggressive form, neuroblastoma. After fourteen months of grueling cancer treatment, we enjoyed eight months of almost "normal" life before he relapsed. Corbin fought his relapse for fourteen more months before leaving us as a perfect fourteen-year-old young man. Despite Corbin's unrelenting treatment schedule that consumed so much of the past four years, he never let that consume him. He lived and loved life one day at a time, was wise beyond his years, and lit up the room with his sweet smile and bright blue eyes. He was our hero and a hero to so many around the world.

Before Corbin's passing, Corbin, his mom, and Corbin's five best friends, who supported him throughout his treatments, founded the C-Squad Foundation, a pediatric cancer foundation dedicated to helping children get the best cancer treatment possible and to supporting promising research aimed at ending cancer in our lifetime. Corbin and his mom will forever be remembered among the dedicated men and women who experienced pain and suffering in this world and were moved to do something about it.

These are all examples of productive anger. Though as you know, anger is not always productive. Anger can be destructive as well. Destructive anger is probably the type of anger that you think about when you think of anger, and it is the type of anger I am attempting to address in this book. But you need to understand that anger, as an emotion, is not bad or wrong. Anger is a natural, God-given response to unjust conditions. It's what you do with anger that can be helpful and productive, or unhelpful and destructive.

Destructive Anger

Destructive anger is the type of anger that does not seek the welfare or charity of another. It seeks harm and revenge. It's unforgiving, vindicative, and unloving. It can be displayed externally in words and actions, or it can be entirely internal, taking a deep root in the heart. In therapy, I'm more concerned about the latter, unless crimes have been committed, as the former is usually easier to address and change. Destructive external anger is the type of anger that everyone can see, and the person often gets in trouble for it. It's the door-slamming, item-throwing, dog-kicking, storm-out-the-door-and-drive-away kind of anger. This person's main problem is a lack of self-control. Usually, this person has been triggered by something within their immediate environment or awareness, and their go-to response is to explode. You can see how destructive external anger can hurt relationships and occupational functioning, depending on when and where it occurs.

And in case destructive external anger appears minimized by the above paragraph, I'll also point out that many of the crimes committed toward people, which victims suffer from and which criminals are in prison for, are crimes committed in this kind of anger. Destructive anger, external or internal, is like a drug; it alters a person's state of mind and can result in behavior that may or may not be out of character for the person. Assault, rape, domestic violence, cyberbullying, child abuse, kidnapping, and homicide are all examples of crimes typically committed in anger.

Destructive internal anger is the type of anger that is not necessarily triggered by something within the person's immediate environment or awareness, though it could be, but it is longer lasting and deep rooted. That is not to say that certain things don't trigger this internal anger response. They do. But I'm speaking here of a person whose default emotion is anger. Most of the time, they stay irritable, sullen, and brooding. They are grumpy, regardless of their situation. A person can become this way when they have experienced a tragic event and have not been able to process it successfully. They have instead become stuck. This stuck-ness has led to deep-rooted anger toward whomever or whatever caused the tragedy. The person's anger is internal, in that they may not lash out with outburst behavior, but their anger is just as real and just as present.

Many years ago, I had an opportunity to work in a workers' compensation clinic providing psychotherapy for people who were injured at work and were suing their employer. The psychotherapy services were mandated by the court, so many individuals did not want to be there. Some of the people there had legitimate injuries that were the fault of the employer. My heart goes out to them and their families concerning the pain or disability they now have to live with. But many of the individuals there seemed to have what could be considered minor injuries or problems that would ordinarily not lead to a loss of work, and it seemed that these individuals wanted to avoid work and get a large sum of lawsuit money from their employer. These individuals were taking advantage of the system by deceit, driven by their greed and laziness.

The individuals in this latter category were, by and large, plagued with destructive internal anger. They hated their employer. Their employer did them wrong in some way, and they were going to *make them pay for it*, literally. Sure, some of them could have engaged in destructive external anger by "going postal," and thankfully that didn't happen too often. But most of them just wanted to sue the pants off someone and make a ton of money. The internal anger was so pronounced that these patients dominated the entirety of each session with complaining, criticizing, accusing, and judging. A deep-rooted bitterness was present that wasn't going to be shaken any time soon, and certainly nothing I could say helped. I didn't work at this clinic for very long!

Like anxiety and depression, anger is a feeling, or emotion, and in most cases, it starts in the mind. That is, it flows from how you think. It's our thoughts that produce feelings like anxiety, depression, and anger. A tragic experience by itself does not produce destructive anger, but how and what we think about the experience can produce it. Corbin, his mom, and their friends were struck with the worst imaginable catastrophic tragedy, yet they turned their anger toward productivity, while some of the individuals I described in the workers' compensation clinic who were struck with a much less severe tragedy turned to destructive anger and bitterness. Anger resulting from tragedy becomes productive or destructive based on how and what we think about the tragic experience.

Anger in the Bible

As we have learned, God does not get anxious or depressed. God can, however, experience a type of anger. God's anger is always the productive type, even when his anger results in wrath on the subjects of his anger. His anger is never purposeless, out of control, or sinful. It would be considered righteous anger, an anger kindled in the same way and by the same definition we have already discussed: Anger is an emotion characterized by antagonism toward someone or something you feel has deliberately done you wrong. While this was the definition we used for anger as it relates to us, I would add a point of clarification as it relates to God: The deliberate wrong to God is the deliberate *sin* by us.

God sees the effects of sin better than anyone else does. We see its effects, but only as much as is evident to human eyes. God sees inside the heart and knows anger's devasting effects on a person's life, relationships, spirituality, and soul. Additionally, we may only see the ramifications of sin in the immediate context. For example, when a husband cheats on his wife, we see the effects on his wife and kids, while God sees the effects on his wife, kids, and generations of children to follow from those kids, along with neighbors, friends, coworkers, and every single person they all will meet that will be impacted by the husband's sin of infidelity. Yes, sin has connections across space and time. And because of God's love for his creation of humanity, and his understanding of the devasting effects of sin on us, sin makes God sad and angry.

There are numerous examples throughout the Bible of God's anger with his people over their sin. God's feeling of anger over sin is real, and results in real wrath. This is evident in both the Old and New Testaments. You may have a hard time wrapping your head around this. How, or why, does God become so angry at sin? To help us understand this a bit better, the analogy of a marriage relationship is a good one, and often used in Scripture. As I write this chapter, my wife and I just celebrated twenty years together. By the grace of God, there has never been infidelity in our marriage. But I think about how I would feel if there had been. Of course, I don't advocate murder, but I can see why we hear stories on the news at times of a husband catching his wife in the act of adultery and murdering both the wife and her lover. While I would like to say I'd never do that, I can see how a husband could go there.

Adultery is how the Bible describes Israel's unfaithfulness toward God. Throughout the Bible, God is described as the husband of the wife Israel, who repeatedly and deliberately cheats on him (Jeremiah 3; Hosea 2; Ezekiel 16). Just as any spouse who is cheated on would be angry, God is angry with Israel when she is unfaithful to him.

I said that God sees the devasting effects of sin. When we, God's children, deliberately commit sin against God's other children, he is not happy with this. As a father, I'm upset when one of my sons deliberately hurts his brother. In the same way, God is upset when he sees this happening between his children. God can feel a special kind of embrace for the weak, lowly, and rejected who are sinned against, and anger toward the sinner for hurting them (Psalm 82:1–4; Jeremiah 21:12). This goes back to the "other side of love" we talked about earlier in this chapter.

But don't get the idea that God is quick to anger, hot-tempered, or angry all the time. Quite the contrary. The Bible describes God as infinitely patient. At least thirteen times in the Bible, God is described as "slow to anger." Psalm 103:8–13 is a great picture of God's mercy, patience, and love.

> The LORD is merciful and gracious,
> > slow to anger and abounding in steadfast love.
> He will not always chide,
> > nor will he keep his anger forever.
> He does not deal with us according to our sins,
> > nor repay us according to our iniquities.
> For as high as the heavens are above the earth,
> > so great is his steadfast love toward those who fear him;
> as far as the east is from the west,
> > so far does he remove our transgressions from us.
> As a father shows compassion to his children,
> > so the LORD shows compassion to those who fear him.

Anger in Relationships

Being in any relationship brings about the possibility that one or both parties in the relationship will be hurt at some point. Think about all the relationships you are in and have ever been in: a son or daughter, a sibling, a friend, a parent, a grandparent, a spouse, a mentor, a student, a coach, or a player. In every relationship, there are opportunities for hurt. It's been said that anger is just the covering for hurt when someone close to you does you wrong. I think there is truth to that. When I am angry at something that someone close to me has done, if I look deeper, it's really hurt that I feel. Yes, I'm angry. But underneath that, I'm hurt.

In the Bible, it seems that God wants us to understand that our connection with him is more than just the Creator and the created. We have a special relationship with him that is described in the New Testament as son or daughter (Romans 8:15), sibling (Hebrews 2:11), friend (John 15:15), spouse (Revelation 19:7), disciple or student (Luke 6:40), and subordinate (John 20:28). In this relationship, there are lots of opportunities for hurt and anger, going both ways. God may become hurt or angry with us, and we may become hurt or angry with God. These emotions are normal in any human-to-human relationship, and they are normal in the God-to-human relationship as well. So it's not if, but when hurt or anger will happen. And how we deal with the hurt or anger makes all the difference.

In the Gospels, we see Jesus become angry with his disciples (Mark 10:14) and the religious leaders (Mark 3:5). We see his disciples angry with each other (Matthew 20:24). We see Paul and Barnabas angry with one another in a "sharp disagreement" (Acts 15:39), and Paul angry with Peter (Galatians 2:11). In the book of Revelation, Jesus is angry with the church in Laodicea (Revelation 3:15–16). The Bible doesn't hide any of this. Anger is going to happen.

Anger and Sin

Anger, as an emotion, is itself *not* a sin. God created our brains to respond in such a way as to produce anger in our body in response to unjust conditions. This is good, and results in good outcomes if used correctly. If used incorrectly, the effects are devasting. How we handle our anger and what we do with it could be sin, both because it hurts others and because it hurts us. Paul clarifies for us in Ephesians 4:26–27 that anger is not a sin: "Be angry and do not sin; do not let the sun go down on your anger, and give no opportunity to the devil." The idea here is *when* you are angry, do not sin. Or, don't sin when you're angry. And we are going to be angry. The feeling of anger at an unjust situation is normal, God-given, and could lead to correction of the unjust condition. But the Bible warns against sinful behavior when we are angry.

It's in this context of sinful anger that James warns us: "Know this, my beloved brothers: let every person be quick to hear, slow to speak, slow to anger; for the anger of man does not produce the righteousness of God" (James 1:19–20). This type of anger, the destructive type, does not produce the righteousness of God. It destroys relationships between people, whom we are called to love (Mark 12:31). There are numerous examples in the Bible of anger used wrongly (e.g., Cain kills Abel, Moses strikes the rock, King Saul tries to kill David, and Saul persecutes the disciples of Jesus). God calls us to process our anger in an appropriate way, leading to a productive use of it, rather than a destructive use.

Anger and Tragedy
Tragedy has the potential for bringing about anger. This anger can be productive or destructive and can vacillate between the two. How you think will determine the type of anger you feel, how much anger you feel, and how long anger resides within you. Changing how you think will change how you feel and how you respond. Rethinking tragedy and suffering, and God in light of your tragedy and suffering, will affect how you feel and respond to your tragedy and suffering. This is not easy. And given what many of us have been taught about God, tragedy, and suffering, it's no wonder that we struggle with this. Rethinking our view of these topics will help in our recovery from the emotional damage we have experienced due to our tragedy.

This concludes the section focused on explaining the three major emotions we feel when our lives are affected by tragedy. We have briefly covered the practical and biblical aspects of each, specifically, how each emotion affects us and those around us, and how God views, reacts, and relates to each emotion, along with how the range of emotions are discussed and experienced by people in the Bible. In the next section, we will take a deep dive into the four main types of tragedies and explore God's perspective on each. Adopting God's perspective on tragedy, that is, seeing tragedy through a biblical lens, will help you process, adjust, and find peace even in the midst of the horrific tragedy you are experiencing.

Journal Questions

1. This chapter started with Matt, the single father of Abigail. How do you think Matt handled the tragedy with his daughter? Was Matt's anger justified? Was his anger the *productive* or *destructive* kind?

2. Matt's anger toward God eventually led him and Abigail to stop attending church, and Matt became an atheist. Is there another way Matt could have begun to see God in light of this tragedy? How could he have thought differently about God that would have led to more peace and a continued faith?

3. Have you experienced a tragedy that you are enraged about? Have you journaled this out? In my early twenties, there were things that happened to me that made me feel like a bomb went off inside me. It was a situation that I was powerless to control or change. All I could do was pray and journal. On the front of my journal, I wrote the words, "Aggression Journal," because that's what it was. I didn't know it at the time, but letting my anger out on those pages helped me process what was going on. The thoughts and feelings were inside me anyway, and writing them out helped. Sure, I talked to my therapist and close friends about what was going on, but I couldn't talk to them all the time. Writing and praying were things I could do any time I wanted to. If you have thoughts and feelings of intense anger, let them out in your journal.

4. If you do have destructive anger, whether external or internal, how can you turn your destructive anger into productive anger? What are some things you can do that will direct your anger in a productive way?

5. Ephesians 4:26–27 says, "Be angry and do not sin; do not let the sun go down on your anger, and give no opportunity to the devil." I explained that this passage describes anger as something we are going to feel, but when we feel it, we should not sin in our anger. What do you think it means to "not let the sun go down on your anger"? And what does it mean to "give no opportunity to the devil"? What does this part of the verse have to do with anger?

Section III:
Finding Peace in
Our Tragedies

CHAPTER 7

Death

The four major tragedies we experience in this life are death, disease, disaster, and despicable evil. I've broken this section up into three chapters. The first is "Death," the second is "Disease and Disaster," and the third is "Despicable Evil." Death includes death in general for any reason. And it includes all death, the death of unborn children and death throughout the lifespan. Disease includes all diseases, illnesses, physical and mental disabilities, and accidents. Disaster includes natural disasters that may lead to death, disease, illness, or disability. Despicable Evil includes all evil, or sin, even the vilest sins, committed by Satan, demons, and people toward other people. Please keep in mind that whole books have been written about each of these subjects. This is my attempt to present you with a brief discussion of each in three chapters.

Each chapter will examine God's control over the tragedy. The word we will use to describe this is *sovereignty*. *Sovereignty* means ultimate, authoritative power over someone or something. It's the total, final, autonomous, and decisive control over a situation and outcome. For God, this is universal and all-encompassing. It will be shown that God is sovereign over death, disease, disaster, and despicable evil. To do this, we will look at many passages of Scripture. What does the Bible say about God's sovereignty over tragedy? When a tragedy happens, many people, including many Christians, ask questions like, "Where was God when that happened?" "Why did God let that happen?" and "Couldn't he have stopped it?" The *why* question is answered in the next section, "Finding Peace in Our Suffering." For now, we will answer the other two.

I believe that a biblical understanding of God's sovereignty over tragedy will lead to a reduction or stabilization of anxiety, depression, and anger during and following tragedy, and a replacement of these challenging emotions with emotions like peace, hope, and joy. God teaches us about his sovereignty over tragedy to encourage us. He wants us to believe and trust in his ultimate, authoritative power over every single tragedy that happens under the sun. There is no tragedy that happens outside his control. Every tragedy that happens, occurs under the decisiveness of an all-loving God who is *for you*. "If God is for us, who can be against us?" (Romans 8:31). This fact is meant to be known, understood, and believed, and should result in comfort and fearlessness for God's people.

Satan Lied

Approximately 105 people die in the world every minute. So by the time you finish this chapter, if you're a fast reader, over 1,500 people will die. That's 6,300 every hour, and over 150,000 every day. This number is staggering. Imagine two average-size NFL stadiums filled with a person in every seat. That's about how many people die every day. Of the 150,000 daily deaths, approximately 16,000 are children. Also staggering. This is a lot of death, and a lot of people left behind to mourn. If every person knows at least four people well, it could be that every day 600,000 more people are mourning the loss of a loved one. When Satan told Eve in the Garden, "You will not surely die" (Genesis 3:4), he lied.

The Centers for Disease Control and Prevention (CDC) estimates that the average life expectancy for people living in the United States is 76.4 years, which is a little under 4,000 weeks. Using this number in my midforties, I've got around 1,500 weeks to go. Not a lot of time. The fact is, our bodies are not made to last very long. They have a 4,000-week shelf life until expiration. Sure, some more, some less. But not much more. Very few people make it to 100.

The four major tragedies have overlaps. Death can be caused by disease, disaster, and despicable evil. If we make it to old age, the cause of death for the vast majority is disease or system failure, that is, our bodies shut down. Early death is often due to disease, though disaster and despicable evil are also causes of early death. There are few guarantees in life. One of them, however, is that you and I are going to die. If you are reading this book, you are going to die. I don't know when or how, but face the fact that you are going to die. I'm not saying anything we don't already know, but it may be good to remind ourselves of this unavoidable conclusion. King Solomon thought it wise that the living should take this fact to heart (Ecclesiastes 7:2).

Fearing Death

Many in our culture seem obsessed with living forever, slowing the aging process, and looking younger than they are. There is a fanatical, sometimes clinically diagnosable, preoccupation with avoiding aging and death. People are intensely afraid of aging and dying, and several phobias are developed because of this fear. *Thanatophobia* is the specific phobia of death and the dying process. *Death anxiety* is another way to say it. Other phobias and anxiety disorders are rooted in the fear of aging, illness, and death. Illness anxiety disorder, or *hypochondriasis*, is one that comes to mind. Other phobias have branches leading back to this fear of death for some people. Fears of flying, driving, choking, being poisoned, heights, weather, and drowning are some of them. People are intensely afraid of being assaulted, shot, having a home invasion, or some other crime committed against them. Others become obsessed with looking a certain way and have intense preoccupations with minor flaws in their appearance that are, in reality, just part of aging.

To soothe our fears, endless products are marketed and stockpiled to increase the length of life or give the appearance of youth.

- Survivalists stock up on endless rounds of ammunition, water, and food in case of a government takeover, foreign invasion, or civil war.

- Surgeries, medications, supplements, therapies, diets, fitness routines, and lotions are aimed to prolong life, slow the aging process, and give the appearance of youth.

- Books, podcasts, YouTube influencers, research, and organizations exist to help us meet these goals.

- A handful of big-tech companies in this space talk about *curing* aging. There's a growing focus on age reversal therapy, where molecules, cells, and genes are altered to reverse aging. *Ammortality* is a word you'll hear more of. It's the idea that, apart from being killed, we can live in our current bodies, without aging, our whole lives, well past 100 years. Bank of America estimates the antiaging movement will be worth $600 billion by 2025,[27] and investors are capitalizing on this market.

It's not only our generation that is attracted to a type of ammortality. The first humans, Adam and Eve, also liked the idea. "You will not surely die," Eve was told. Yet she, Adam, and everyone else in the Bible—except for maybe Enoch and Elijah, who were taken straight to heaven—died. Since "in Adam all die" (1 Corinthians 15:22), we know that our time here on earth is finite. Even if we prolong life past 100 years, we haven't accomplished anything that hasn't been done before. From Adam to Noah, the shortest life and death record in the Bible is Lamech, who lived 777 years (Genesis 5:31). In the next chapter in Genesis, God put a limit on the span of human life at 120 years (Genesis 6:3). It seems that now God has limited most lives to less than that (Psalms 90:10).

What should the human body's finiteness do for our thinking? Moses, who himself lived to be 120 years old (Deuteronomy 34:7), said it best, "So teach us to number our days that we may get a heart of wisdom" (Psalm 90:12). Knowing that we will not live forever, that we have a very limited amount of time here, and that we are not promised tomorrow helps us make rational choices with our life and use our time productively and meaningfully. It should also help us consider what is beyond this mortal life. A full discussion of these considerations is beyond the scope of this chapter; however, I will close this part with saying that the reality of death, our own and that of others, should give us great pause in our lives so that we think about eternity. God wants us to know with a deep conviction that this life is not all there is. The more we realize that death is inevitable and closer today than it was yesterday, the more we consider what's coming after, and that should hopefully draw us closer to the one who holds life and death in the palm of his hand.

Ownership

The Christian view of life and death is not a popular one, given our independent, "Don't tell me what to do" nature. It has to do with ownership. My wife and I own the home we live in, and therefore have the right to do with it whatever we want. We can paint it, swap out the flooring, replace the kitchen cabinets, etc. We could decorate it with nice furniture and decor, or we could punch holes in the walls and leave trash all over the place. We could even demo the entire house and rebuild a new one. We can do this because we own the house. If my neighbor came over during a remodel and said he didn't like what we were doing to our house, I think I would say, "Thank you for your opinion," while thinking, "Dude, mind your own business; it's *my* house." If we rented our house to tenants, they could *not* do whatever they wanted to it.

It is a hard thing for Westerns to accept, but God *owns* us. Psalm 24:1 says, "The earth is the Lord's and the fullness thereof, the world and those who dwell therein." Did you catch that? "Those who dwell therein" belong to the Lord. All humans, whether we like it or not, belong to God. Therefore, God has the right to do with us as he pleases.

Why does God own us? Because he gave us life, even at the moment of conception. The Old Testament speaks of God opening and closing the womb. God opened Leah's womb, while Rachel's womb remained barren (Genesis 29:31). God closed Hannah's womb (1 Samuel 1:5) until she conceived Samuel (1 Samuel 1:20). Abraham and Sarah could not conceive until God said it was time (Genesis 21:1–2). In the New Testament, Elizabeth considered her conception of John the Baptist as something "the Lord has done for me" (Luke 1:25). God himself says it in Isaiah 66:9: "'Shall I bring to the point of birth and not cause to bring forth?' says the Lord; 'shall I, who cause to bring forth, shut the womb?' says your God."

We have life because God chose to give it to us (Acts 17:25). But it was not a giving that *relinquished* ownership. It was a giving that *maintained* ownership, almost like a rental property. God has given us these bodies to use on earth for a predetermined time. Then, when he's ready, the rental contract expires, and he takes back what is his, "for all that is in the heavens and in the earth is [his]" (1 Chronicles 29:11). And if we are Christians, we doubly belong to God (Romans 14:8; 1 Corinthians 6:19; 2 Corinthians 1:21–22). Hopefully, we have determined in our mind that we were his all along; otherwise, we will be very surprised on judgment day.

And because he gives life, he can take it whenever and however he pleases. God says in Deuteronomy 32:39:

> "See now that I, even I, am he,
>   and there is no god beside me;
> I kill and I make alive;
>   I wound and I heal;
>   and there is none that can deliver out of my hand."

God makes alive and God decides when that life is over; even the number of our days is determined by God (Job 14:5; Psalm 139:16; Acts 17:26). God gives us life, decides how many days we'll be alive, and then takes our life when and how he pleases. When Ephesians 1:11 says that God "works all things according to the counsel of his will," "all things" includes the life and death of every person.

Walking in a Graveyard

My kids think it's weird that I like taking prayer walks in cemeteries. I mean, don't get me wrong, I like the beaches, mountains, and hillsides. Those are great places for a good prayer walk too. But nothing really beats a cemetery. You haven't really prayed until you've prayed in a cemetery. I'm kidding about that last sentence. But seriously, there's something about talking to God while walking through an area with corpses and tombstones all around you. And the older and less well-kept the cemetery, the better. Fairhaven Memorial Park & Mortuary in Santa Ana, California was my place to encounter God from 2012 to 2017. It was a few minutes from my office, and I often took lunch breaks to walk and talk with God in that cemetery. It was a sobering, ominous, and clarifying experience.

This cemetery was opened in 1911, spans seventy-three acres, and is the final resting place for hundreds of thousands of people, many of whom were born in the 1800s. Civil war veterans, the wife of Jim Morrison from The Doors, the creator of Fender guitars, and Corrie ten Boom, the Dutch watchmaker who hid Jews from the Nazis during World War II, are buried there. There are graves of people my age, much older, and much younger. There are graves of babies who lived only one year, and graves of people who lived to be over 100. Some of the graves have a word or two about the person: "Beloved Mother," "Loving Father," "Adored Son." One just says, "Baby," with no name or dates. Some of the tombstones have pictures engraved into them representing a person's passion or interest. One tombstone has a picture of a red Corvette on it.

The immense grounds seem to be organized by the socioeconomic status of the people who are buried, meaning there is definitely a poor area and a wealthy area. The poor area is filled with small plots in the ground, some of them right near a curb and heaving up because of the pavement of the street. The tombstones or plaques are faded, some beyond recognition, and some broken by the roots underneath. The graves are crowded, and the area surrounding them receives minimal attention from the maintenance crew. The wealthy area is bright, spacious, and well kept. There are large, private estate areas for whole families to be buried, decorative single-corpse, walk-in mausoleums, and pristine cathedral-like mausoleums, all to bury the wealthiest residents of Orange County.

As I walked through the streets of this massive burial ground, I couldn't help but think that this same fate awaits *me*. One day, I will be in the ground or in a wall somewhere. It's inevitable. And there will be a tombstone or plaque with my name on it, the day I was born, and the day I died. And I'm talking now, as I walk, to the God who's in control of all that. But as I looked at the decorative mausoleum and the tiny plot in the ground that's coming up because of street cement or tree roots, I thought, *"What does it really matter?"* Whether my remains end up in a fancy, private estate or a hole in the ground matters very little compared to where my *soul* wakes up after I close my mortal eyes for the last time.

The other clarifying lesson that occurred during these prayer walks is that God has final, decisive control over the exact second when someone's life ends and the circumstance that brings about that end. Just like he has final, decisive control over birth, he has final, decisive control over death. The name and two dates on each tombstone were decided by God before the person was born. As I looked at the names, I realized that all these people lived and breathed and walked and talked, just like I'm doing right now. They had jobs, families, friends, worries, and dreams. And now, all that's over. They were given life by God, and he took it when he decided it was time.

Who Controls Death?

The biblical authors understood who was in control of death. "The Lord kills and brings to life; he brings down to Sheol and raises up" (1 Samuel 2:6). "No man has power to retain the spirit, or power over the day of death" (Ecclesiastes 8:8). Today we question this. But in the minds of the people in the Bible, it was clear. Even when a great wind struck the house that Job's children were in and they died, Job attributed the final, decisive cause to God: "The Lord gave, and the Lord has taken away; blessed be the name of the Lord" (Job 1:21). And in case we question whether Job unjustly attributed this action to God, the narrator of Job makes it clear in the next verse that he did not: "In all this Job did not sin or charge God with wrong" (Job 1:22).

But I thought Satan was responsible for the death of Job's children? He was. Satan can and does have a level of causality in some deaths. As a "murderer from the beginning" (John 8:44), Satan comes to "steal and kill and destroy" (John 10:10). But as John Piper says in his book *Providence*,[28] Satan's causality in death is not ultimate or decisive. Satan's power over death, and everything for that matter, is always on a leash. Additionally, natural causes, unnatural accidents, sinful human choices and actions, our own choices and actions, and even our foolishness may have levels of causality in death, but none of these are ultimate or decisive. God holds the final, decisive authority to decide what ultimately causes death. We'll talk more about some of this in the next two chapters.

Finally, consider the words of James:

Come now, you who say, "Today or tomorrow we will go into such and such a town and spend a year there and trade and make a profit"—yet you do not know what tomorrow will bring. What is your life? For you are a mist that appears for a little time and then vanishes. Instead you ought to say, "If the Lord wills, we will live and do this or that." As it is, you boast in your arrogance. All such boasting is evil. (James 4:13–16)

What do you think about the person who says, "Today or tomorrow we will go into such and such a town and spend a year there and trade and make a profit"? That sounds like pretty normal talk in our world, right? We make our plans and decide when and where we'll go and what we'll do there. I have counseled hundreds of young adults in my practice who think like this. I was one who thought like this, and still can if I'm not careful. This kind of thinking aligns perfectly with the God-absent, human-centered society we have created, but it does not align with Scripture.

If the Lord wills, we will live. If the Lord does not will that we live, we will not. I've been called a lot of things in my life, but a "mist" is quite insulting. I mean, really? I am a fully rational, intelligent human being with ideas, motivations, feelings, actions, and relationships. I'm not a mist. Yes, I am. And so are you. We all are. Most of us just don't know it. The "little time" we are here before vanishing is just that. We're here, then we're gone. And the only people who never question this reality are the people I walked by in the cemetery who were already in the ground.

How Should We Feel?
In this chapter, we've concisely discussed the relative brevity of life and unpredictability of death, God's ownership of our lives, and his sovereignty over life and death. How should this make us feel? That's my interest as a psychologist and is the area I feel most qualified to address. For this answer, we'll look to Jesus.

Loss by Tragedy

Many of us have experienced the loss of a loved one due to horrific, sinful tragedy. What could be more tragic in Jesus' life than the death of his cousin, John the Baptist? In Chapter 9 of this book, we'll discuss more specifically the tragedy of despicable evil. For now, we'll briefly look at Jesus' response to one instance of it in his own life. John was six months older than Jesus, and while growing up they lived quite a distance from each other, but they would likely have seen each other and spent time together at least once a year during Passover in Jerusalem. It's speculation, but I think they may have seen each other even more often. I mean, Mary traveled approximately 100 miles pregnant through a desert to see John's mom! Also speculation, but it's also possible that John and Jesus had a lot in common, and maybe even talked about their hopes and dreams for the kingdom of God. So they were cousins *and* friends.

At some point, they parted ways. It's thought that John went to live in an obscure desert region with the Essenes, a Jewish sect that strove for holiness by ascetical practices, while Jesus stayed in Nazareth and took on the family business. John's ministry was to prepare the way for his cousin, the Messiah. When John went public with his ministry, he baptized Jesus in the Jordan River. Jesus spoke highly of John in Matthew 11:11, stating that John was the greatest man ever born. That's quite a compliment coming from the Son of God! By this point, John had been arrested by King Herod for preaching against Herod's adulterous behavior. What happens next is atrocious.

In prison, John was beheaded at the command of Herod, following the request of the daughter of Herodias, Herod's sister-in-law, whom Herod also married. After a dance performed by Herodias's daughter on Herod's birthday for Herod and his guests, Herod promised her a gift of whatever she wanted, even "up to half of my kingdom" (Mark 6:23). At the prompting of her mother, the daughter of Herodias requested John's head on a platter. To save face in front of his guests, Herod gave in. Think about this for a minute. The greatest man who ever lived, the cousin of Jesus, a man in his early thirties with much life ahead of him for the kingdom of God, died in a most unnecessary, senseless, and brutal manner. What was Jesus' response?

Let's first talk about what Jesus did *not* do. He did not storm the castle, protest John's unfair, needless execution, or kill Herod. Jesus did not publicly condemn Herod for his hasty, sinful actions. Jesus did not discontinue his ministry of preaching and teaching or stop preaching against adultery. Jesus did not lose sight of his goals, abandon his mission, or neglect the people who needed him.

What *did* Jesus do? Matthew 14:13 says what Jesus did when he heard about John's death. "Now when Jesus heard this, he withdrew from there in a boat to a desolate place by himself." Jesus wanted silence and solitude. He wanted to get away, not forever, but for a time. Away from the crowds, the commotion, and from the needs of ministry. He wanted to think, pray, and process what happened. He did what he did every morning: "And rising very early in the morning, while it was still dark, he departed and went out to a desolate place, and there he prayed" (Mark 1:35). Jesus wanted to be alone with God. We need this too. When a tragedy happens, it's important to stop and get time in silence and solitude to process what happened. It's hard to do this when your day-to-day is filled with noise, activity, and people.

But as you know, Jesus didn't get what he wanted. The next sentence in the same verse says, "But when the crowds heard it, they followed him on foot from the towns" (Matthew 14:13). Jesus gets where he is going and finds a large crowd waiting for him. I don't know about you, but this would have been the last thing I wanted to see. When I'm hurting, I need space. Jesus may have felt the same way, but he didn't show it. That part didn't come out. He didn't demand "me time." Instead, "When he went ashore he saw a great crowd, and he had compassion on them and healed their sick" (Matthew 14:14). In Jesus' sorrow over the death of his cousin, he listened to God. That is, he observed the situation objectively, coming out of his own internal battle within himself, and reasoned that the needs of these people should take priority over his feelings.

It says that Jesus had "compassion." Maybe he said something to himself like, *"I'm hurting, but they are hurting more. And they don't have a way to deal with their pain. I'm their way. I won't let them down. My pain, though real, can wait."* In meeting the needs of others, it's likely Jesus' needs were met too. Have you ever been hurt, but in your pain decided to be around people, listen to their problems, or serve them in some way? I have. After listening to the hurts and pains of others, and serving people in need, somehow my problems seem less daunting, less troubling. Not that Jesus did it for this reason, but this opportunity to help others may have been exactly what Jesus needed during that painful hour.

And Jesus did get his time. After performing one of his greatest miracles, the feeding of the 5,000, he dismissed his disciples and the crowds, and "he went up on the mountain by himself to pray. When evening came, he was there alone" (Matthew 14:23). Finally, time with God alone to pray. If you've ever longed for time alone with God and didn't get it for a while, when it finally comes, it's amazing. The mind and heart in a state of deprivation can only be filled one way, and that way is God. And we know Jesus was alone with God on that mountain for a while. It says in Matthew 14:25 that he went to his disciples in the "fourth watch of the night." That's between 3:00am and 6:00am. So, pretty much all night in unbroken time with God. This is what Jesus needed, and it's what we sometimes need as well.

Loss by Illness

Like many of us, Jesus lost someone to illness. As I think about the people I've lost in my life, most of them were lost to some incurable illness or disease. My wife and I have known a lot of couples who have had miscarriages, that is, babies who die before they are born. We have known some families who have experienced the death of a child, spouse, or friend due to illness. I think the lessons learned from Jesus in response to the death of his friend Lazurus can help us in any of these situations described.

First, we need to understand what death is. Death, according to the Bible, is a *general* result, or consequence, of sin, though not always the sin of the person who dies. This is most certainly not the case for babies or children who die. I mean sin in general and of this fallen world we live in. Sin is a product of the fallen, decaying world, ever since Adam and Eve were expelled from the Garden. God told them this would happen (Genesis 2:17). And we have all inherited a sinful nature from our first parents, Adam and Eve. The Apostle Paul explains this in Romans 5:12:

"Therefore, just as sin came into the world through one man, and death through sin, and so death spread to all men because all sinned."

Second, death is God's enemy and will be destroyed. 1 Corinthians 15:26 says, "The last enemy to be destroyed is death." Death is God's enemy because death is the product of sin (Romans 6:23). In the future, when God puts all things right, he will destroy forever sin and death. Death has power over us now (though death is still under the power of God), but it will not have power over us forever. "Death is swallowed up in victory" (1 Corinthians 15:54). The victory of Jesus Christ is that he overcame death in his own life, and he will overcome death for all who put their faith in him. Yes, our mortal bodies will die, but our souls will not. Jesus said, "Whoever believes in me, though he die, yet shall he live, and everyone who lives and believes in me shall never die" (John 11:25–26). Our soul will live on in eternity with Jesus because death will not have power over it.

Third, in a way, death is our friend. Death is the only way we will have a direct, face to face, perfect connection with Jesus, and a perfectly sinless existence. Until then, what we have in our relationship with Jesus is imperfect, and our bodies are riddled with sin, even though as we live, we are forgiven. This is why Paul said, "For to me to live is Christ, and to die is gain" (Philippians 1:21). Paul wanted to stay here to continue his fruitful ministry, but he wanted more to be face to face with the living Christ. Living was good, if to live is Christ. But dying was "far better" (Philippians 1:23).

While we live, we have to face the reality of death in our own mortal bodies and others. Some will die peacefully in their sleep after a long, fruitful life of service to Christ with their loving family surrounding them, and some will die alone, much younger, in complete agony, and with far fewer accomplishments. Either case will be true for Christians and non-Christian, adults and children. So, what can we learn from Jesus' experience of his friend dying?

Space evades us in this chapter to describe this account of Jesus, Lazarus, Mary, and Martha. But I will say a few things. First, when Jesus saw people weeping over Lazarus's death, and when he came to Lazarus tomb, he was "deeply moved" (John 11:33). This phrase in Greek carries with it a kind of indignation. There was provoking of Jesus that was more than sadness. As Jesus surveyed the scene, he may have had in mind the reality of death as the enemy and the devastation this enemy brings, and especially how it impacted his dear friends, Mary and Martha. This deeply troubled him. Second, Jesus wept (John 11:35). It was not just indignation felt by Jesus. He was also very sad. Jesus did not hold back tears in the presence of all the people there. He expressed his sadness openly. Jesus shows us that feelings of indignation and sadness are appropriate when someone we love dies, and that there are times when it's ok to express them openly. Third, although Jesus himself was grieving, he was able to comfort the sisters. Fourth, even though Jesus knew he could and would raise Lazarus from the dead, it did not stop him from being in the moment with his grief, and with the sisters.

Fear Not
Finally, Jesus tells us to not fear those who could kill us. In Matthew 10, Jesus is talking to his disciples about persecution and specifies who we should and should not fear: "And do not fear those who kill the body but cannot kill the soul. Rather fear him who can destroy both soul and body in hell" (Matthew 10:28). Jesus then explains why. "Are not two sparrows sold for a penny? And not one of them will fall to the ground apart from your Father. But even the hairs of your head are all numbered. Fear not, therefore; you are of more value than many sparrows (Matthew 10:29-31). Jesus describes that not even the death of a tiny, insignificant, almost worthless sparrow in the most remote part of the world happens apart from God's will. And disciples of Jesus are of much more value to God than sparrows. And even the very hairs on our head are numbered. God knows and wills the smallest, most insignificant details of our lives. If he knows and wills the small things, he also knows and wills the big things.

Our command is to "fear not." As we may seek solitude, weep, and become indignant over death, let us never fear. God has the tiniest details of our lives in the palm of his hand. And he has an even more glorious reality waiting for us, our children, and our loved ones beyond this life, where "he will wipe away every tear from their eyes, and death shall be no more, neither shall there be mourning, nor crying, nor pain anymore, for the former things have passed away" (Revelation 21:4).

As we close this chapter, keep in mind that the messages about death in the Bible are not going to cure you of your pain automatically. I'm not even sure that *curing* is the goal. These teachings are meant to aid in the healing process, as you think and pray through them. Over time, God will bring you to a place of peace as you consider the realities of death and the responses of God, Jesus, and others presented in this chapter. Don't give up hope on your pursuit of peace. Grieving is a natural experience when a loved one dies. Don't rush the process. Jesus grieved, and he knows your pain. He is there to comfort you and understands how hard it is to carry on when someone you love passes on. In the next chapter, we will consider loss due to other tragedies: disease and disaster.

Journal Questions

1. How can a belief in the sovereignty of God over death help us as we process the loss of a loved one?

2. Do you fear death? How much do you think about death and what behaviors do you engage in to avoid death? Is a fear or preoccupation with death necessary or rational when you consider God's sovereignty over death? How should God's sovereignty over death settle our fears?

3. I highly recommend taking a walk in a graveyard. If you have the opportunity, plan a time to do this. When you are there, pray, watch, and think. Then, in your car or when you get home, write in your journal about your experience. What did you think and feel as you walked along? How did this experience affect how you view life and death?

4. In this chapter, I discussed Jesus' response to two of his friends dying: One died from the despicable sin of others, and one due to illness. Read through those sections again, and the corresponding passages in the Bible, to really grasp how Jesus responded to these deaths. Are there ways that Jesus responded to

the deaths of his friends that you can implement in your own life?

5. Paul said, "For to me to live is Christ, and to die is gain" (Philippians 1:21) and essentially that departing (dying) is "far better" than living since he would be with Christ when he died (Philippians 1:23). This is a radical mindset shift from our normal way of thinking, and the thinking in our culture. How would adopting this mindset help us have peace in our thinking about death?

CHAPTER 8

Disease and Disaster

The sounds were familiar: moaning, crying, yelling, and "happy" sounds. I was walking up to the home of six men with severe to profound intellectual disabilities. It was a nice, middle class family neighborhood near the beach in Southern California. But inside was different from the other homes in the neighborhood. This home was owned by the State of California and funded by the Department of Developmental Disabilities. While in graduate school, I worked as a case manager, and later as a behavior consultant, for an agency that provided services to children and adults with developmental disabilities, including intellectual disabilities, Down syndrome, cerebral palsy, epilepsy, and autism spectrum disorder. During this time, I saw and learned things that would change how I see the world forever.

Not everyone with a developmental disability lived in a state-funded house with paid staff. Some lived in hospital settings or institutions. But most lived at home with their family. The push by the State was to have people remain in their homes with as much support as possible. It made sense. Independence, opportunities, family relationships, and quality of life were all things that were enhanced by normalcy and a least-restrictive living environment. Sometimes *least-restrictive living* meant that the person needed around-the-clock caretaking. Depending on the individual, *caretaking* could have meant physical, medical, behavioral, or all three. Let me give you some examples.

People with profound intellectual disability have living skills equivalent to about a three-year-old child and have little to no functional speech. Many function at a lower age than three. Jeff is in his twenties and has a full-time caregiver sitting next to him all day to wipe his drool, change his diaper, and block his hand from hitting his head every thirty seconds or so. Frances is in her forties and has a full-time caregiver to prevent her from smearing feces on herself and surfaces around the house. Michael is in his thirties and can't get up from his bed, so he needs to be turned in his bed every two hours to prevent bed sores, and he is fed from a feeding tube. Lindsey is fourteen years old, blind, nonverbal, and can't walk, so she scoots around the house on her back. Jason is ten years old and has no functional skills, so he sits in a stroller all day and watches television.

Not everyone I worked with had disabilities at this level. Many were much higher functioning, but they exhibited some extreme behaviors. Because of their disabilities, they lacked emotional control and social skills, and were highly reactive. As a behavior consultant, my job was to design plans to help reduce behaviors like self-injury, aggression, and outbursts, and teach functional skills to replace these behaviors, such as some form of communication and calming strategies. Janis was seven years old and would violently slap herself in the face, pull her hair out, and throw herself on the ground at the slightest hint that she was not going to get her way. One of my most difficult cases was Trevor, who was sixteen years old. When I met him for the first time, he was standing in the middle of his apartment living room with six guys around him wearing protective fight gear. He was agitated, and I was told that at any second he could lunge at someone and attack without warning or any observable trigger.

I could go on and on, but I think you get the picture. As a young man, I was faced with a reality next door that I wasn't aware of. Most of these people were born this way and were not going to get much better. The saddest ones, though, were the people who had lived a normal life for many years, and then due to a severe traumatic brain injury or an illness that affected their brain, became this way. As a Christian, how was I to make sense of this? Here I was with all the capacities and resources available to me to do almost anything I wanted. And here was Michael, a man my age, unable to feed himself due to no fault of his own.

God "heals all your diseases" (Psalm 103:3). What does this mean for Michael, Jeff, Frances, Lindsey, Jason, and countless others who live with disease, illness, and disability? And what does this mean for their parents, who have had their lives permanently altered the moment they gave birth to a child with a disability? This chapter deals with all types of disease, illness, disability, and accidents, along with natural disasters that can lead to disease, illness, disability, and even death.

The Problem

I stated the obvious in the last chapter: We are all going to die. We know that the human body is not meant to last forever. There are only so many heartbeats that will happen before the last. Most of us, likely, wish that it will beat for eighty-plus years and will only stop once we've done everything we want to do, without any pain or discomfort, and in our sleep. Woody Allen said, "I'm not afraid to die, I just don't want to be there when it happens." Unfortunately, we don't know when or how it will happen. No one wants to get a disease or illness that leads to their death, or maybe worse, a lifetime of pain or disability. We're all on the same page here.

However, the world we live in makes no such promises. On the contrary, it's possible that many of us will develop some disease, or illness, or have a disaster occur that leaves us in a different condition than before, and for some, it will result in death. MalaCards, the human disease database, lists 44,000 diseases across two sections: anatomical diseases (e.g., blood, bone, immune, muscle, and reproductive) and global diseases (cancer, fetal, genetic, infectious, and metabolic).[29] The Centers for Disease Control and Prevention (CDC) estimates that 27 percent of North American adults have a disability.[30] Autism affects 1 in 36 children, according to the most recent reports.[31] Blindness, deafness, paralysis, and more are present across the globe. Disease and disabilities are rampant.

For as many actions as we are able to accomplish, each one has a potential accident waiting to happen. A long time ago, I remember watching someone move a large, old-school television from a table with a baby in a car seat on the ground next to the table. The person fumbled the television, and it almost fell on top of the baby. Thankfully, the person caught the television right before it fell, as it would have certainly crushed the baby and either killed him or severely disabled him, changing his and his parents' lives forever. But many people are not that fortunate. People get electrocuted while taking a walk, fall off roofs setting up Christmas decorations, drown in pools, get limbs mangled in dangerous machinery, and get in car accidents every day. These life-altering, sometimes life-ending accidents leave us and others devastated and perplexed. Accidents are rampant.

The Federal Emergency Management Agency (FEMA) lists eighteen natural hazards (disasters) that occur, including avalanche, coastal flooding, cold wave, drought, earthquake, hail, heat wave, hurricane, ice storm, landslide, lightning, riverine flooding, strong wind, tornado, tsunami, volcanic activity, wildfire, and winter weather.[32] Fifteen of these, including fires, floodings, storms, and tornadoes, have occurred in the United States in the first three months of 2024. These disasters often leave behind emotional, physical, and financial damage that some people never recover from. Natural disasters are rampant.

There is neither time, space, ability, nor necessity to cover every single disease, disability, illness, accident, or disaster that plagues human experience daily and worldwide. It is sufficient to say that we live in a world of catastrophic enormity. Even in my own short life, my dad's mental illness resulted in his suicide, I was diagnosed with MS, and my wife was diagnosed with epilepsy. Not to mention all the funerals we've attended, with causes ranging from car crashes to heart attacks to breast cancer. And many of you have experienced tragedies in this category a million times worse.

Is Any of This Mentioned in the Bible?
The Bible is not silent in the areas of disease, illness, accident, and disaster. In fact, it seems that the Bible screams at us with these kinds of tragedies from start to finish. I've listed a very small portion of them here:

Disease and Illness

- Pestilence (plague) is mentioned in fourteen of the Old Testament books and is brought by the pale horse of Revelation 6.

- 70,000 men died from pestilence following King David's sin (1 Chronicles 21:14).

- Cases of leprosy occur frequently in the Bible. Naaman, a Syrian army commander, had leprosy (2 Kings 5:1), and leper colonies were present throughout the Old and New Testaments. Jesus healed several lepers (e.g., Luke 17:11–17).

- King Jehoram suffered with a type of bowel disease that caused him to die in "great agony" (2 Chronicles 21:18–19).

- King Asa had a disease in his feet (2 Chronicles 16:12).

- Loathsome sores covered Job's body (Job 2:7).

- Jesus healed a lot of people with diseases (Matthew 4:23), including a woman with blood hemorrhaging for twelve years (Luke 8:43) and a boy with seizures (Matthew 17:15).

Disability and Accidents

- Isaac was blind (Genesis 27:1).

- Jacob walked with a limp (Genesis 32:25).

- Moses claimed to be "slow of speech and of tongue" (Exodus 4:10).

- King Saul's grandson, Mephibosheth, couldn't walk due to a permanent injury of his feet from being dropped as a small child (2 Samuel 4:4).

- King Ahaziah fell from his balcony and was seriously injured (2 Kings 1:2).

- Zacchaeus may have had a disability that affected his height (Luke 19:3).

- Jesus encountered many people who were blind, deaf, mute, paralyzed, or in some other way disabled, including the man born blind (John 9:1), the man with a withered hand in Mark 3, and the woman who was "bent over and could not fully straighten herself" for eighteen years (Luke 13:11).

Disaster

- We don't get too far into human history before the entire world's population, save Noah and his seven family members, are killed in a catastrophic flood (Genesis 6–7).

- Abraham and Isaac each experienced at least one famine (Genesis 12:10, 26:1) before the famine that affected Egypt and surrounding countries in Joseph's time (Genesis 41:53–57).

- Famines occur throughout the Bible (e.g., Ruth 1:1; 2 Samuel 21:1; 2 Kings 8:1).

- The plagues of Egypt were catastrophic disasters (Exodus 7–11).

- Wind struck the corners of the house Job's children were in, and they died (Job 1:19).

- Jesus spoke about a tower in Siloam that fell, killing eighteen people (Luke 13:4), and predicted famines and earthquakes as a sign of the end of the age (Matthew 24:7).

- The Book of Revelation is filled with descriptions of disasters that come upon the earth, more than we have space to mention. It describes hail and fire thrown upon the earth, burning up a third of the earth and the trees and all the green grass (Revelation 8:7), and a third of the world's drinking water becoming toxic (Revelation 8:11).

Ultimate Authority

Disease, illness, disability, accident, and disaster as described above are part of the fallen world we live in. The whole world is under bondage to corruption as it groans in the pains of childbirth (see Romans 8:20–23). But not everyone suffers the same. Some live with diseases and disabilities and some do not. Some suffer from immense disaster, and some do not. Many of us know people who are comfortable and free from any real complaints, and others who can't get through a single day without pain or suffering of some kind. God does not promise us long life, comfort, prosperity, or a life free from agony, despite what the prosperity preachers tell us. Even our Lord himself healed many, but not all who were disabled or sick in the region of Galilee (Mark 1:34) and promised that in this world we will have tribulation (John 16:33).

I presented a few examples above to show that the Bible is no stranger to these kinds of tragedies. But why is all of this in there? One reason is because the Bible presents real life. The tragedies mentioned in the Bible are real, affecting real people, and really possible for any of us today. The examples of tragic events in the Bible have various causes. In some of the examples, we are told who, or what, caused them. In others, we are not. For example, God sent the famine during Joseph's life (Psalm 105:16–17), the plagues of Egypt (Exodus 7–11), and the plague that struck the Israelites in the wilderness (Numbers 11:33). Satan struck Job with loathsome sores (Job 2:7) and kept the woman bound in her disability (Luke 13:16). An angel of the Lord struck Herod, and he was eaten by worms (Acts 12:23). Mephibosheth was dropped by his nurse (2 Samuel 4:4). Isaac was blind due to old age (Genesis 27:1). Possibly poor engineering of the tower, bad weather, or both killed the people of Siloam (Luke 13:4). We don't know how Lazurus got sick (John 11:1) or how the man in John 9 was born blind.

I said we don't know how they got sick or were born blind. But that was only a half-truth. We do know ultimately who was decisive in their illness and disability, and therefore at least part of the *how* is answered. God, who saw their unborn body and determined their every day before one of them came to be (Psalm 139:16), said to Moses, "Who has made man's mouth? Who makes him mute, or deaf, or seeing, or blind? Is it not I, the Lord?" (Exodus 4:11). We may not know the intermediate cause, but we do know the final, or ultimate, cause. An intermediate cause is a cause (e.g., something visible or invisible like Satan, a person, a virus, natural deterioration, the wind, an earthquake, hail, a virus, etc.) that happens *in between* God's final determination of a situation or event to happen. This will make more sense shortly.

There may be several intermediate causes of diseases and disasters. Some we can know and some we cannot know. But regardless of the intermediate cause, one thing we know for certain: God is sovereign over all of them. I think that is why so much disease and disaster are shown in the Bible. Disease and disaster have always been a major part of every generation and surely will be for the remainder of humanity. The Bible gives us ample information and evidence to show that God is the final, decisive[33] authority over all of it. Even when there is an intermediary cause, like Satan, the wind, worms, viruses, or poor planning, we can rest in God's ultimate authority over all of it. So, in the current diseases and disasters we are experiencing, we either don't know the intermediary cause, or we do, but either way, we know that God is ultimately in control of the final decision of our situation.

God's decisive power reigns over all tragedy and suffering on earth. The examples of tragedy in the Bible are there to show God's sovereignty over them. If God is not sovereign over these tragedies, then who or what is? Satan? Humankind? Nature? Or maybe there is no sovereign power over tragedy. Maybe everything is random and subject to chance. If we believe the Bible, we can't believe that Satan, humankind, nature, or chance have the final say. The Bible presents God as having final, ultimate, decisive authority over tragedy of all kinds. This ultimate authority, or sovereignty, is the final call. The final say. The buck has to stop somewhere, and that somewhere is God.

Job

Another way to say this is that God has ultimate *causality* in disease, illness, accidents, disaster, and disability. Sure, there are other, intermediary causes. But as I mentioned here and in the last chapter concerning death, not one of these causes is final or decisive. There are levels of causality when it comes to tragedy. Job, for example, had a tidal wave of calamities happen to him, some of which were of the type we're describing in this chapter. I've mentioned the "great wind" that struck the house Job's children were in so that they all died (Job 1:19) and the "loathsome sores" that covered Job's body, causing excruciating pain (Job 2:7).

To illustrate God's ultimate authority over tragedies in this category, I will use an example from the Book of Job. Not every disease and disaster that occurs in life has Satan's hand in it, but when it does, I want to show God's sovereignty even over situations where the worst, vilest creature is involved. If God is sovereign even over our enemy, and when our enemy attacks us, then maybe we can accept that he is sovereign over other intermediary causes, like natural causes and human agency. The Book of Job shows God's sovereignty even over Satanic causes.

And if we use Job as a model for suffering, which I think we can do, since even James did so in his book (James 5:11), we see that suffering from great tragedy has nothing to do with the person's faith or righteousness (Job 1:1, 8), meaning that some people of great faith and righteousness suffer immensely, while some do not, and at the same time, some people with no faith and great wickedness suffer immensely, while some do not. The amount of faith a person has is not a necessary condition for suffering or ease, but it's the purposes of God in the suffering that prevail above all.

Wind and The Death of Job's Children
I can't even begin to imagine losing a child. I remember attending the funeral of a friend of our family who died in a car accident at the age of twenty-three. Afterward, at the wake, his parents were utterly inconsolable. They lost their precious son before he really got to live, and they would spend the rest of their lives without him. Job lost all ten of his children instantly in a single tragic event. "A great wind came across the wilderness and struck the four corners of the house, and it fell upon the young people, and they are dead" (Job 1:19). That's it. Here one second and gone the next.

How can we explain their death? If you recall, God and Satan had a conversation right before this happened. In this conversation, God mentioned Job to Satan, not the other way around: "And the Lord said to Satan, 'Have you considered my servant Job?'" (Job 1:8). Satan then challenged God regarding Job, saying that Job only feared God because God had put a divine hedge around him and blessed his life. Satan then challenged God to "stretch out *your* hand and touch all that he has, and he will curse you to your face" (Job 1:11, emphasis mine). Satan dared God to stretch out his own hand toward Job and do something that would cause Job to curse God.

Something interesting happens next. God doesn't say, "No," and he doesn't say, "Ok, I'll do it" or "All right, watch this." Like, "I trust that my servant Job will pass the test, so here we go." Instead, God says to Satan, "Behold, all that he has is in *your* hand. Only against him do not stretch out your hand" (Job 1:12, emphasis mine). Then, several tragedies happen, one of which is the wind striking the house Job's children are in.

I've heard it said that Satan asked God for *permission* to test Job. I don't see that here. This doesn't mean that Satan never asks permission (e.g., Luke 22:31), but what I see in Job is God telling Satan about Job ("Have you considered my servant Job?"), and Satan *challenging* God to test Job. Satan doesn't ask God for permission to strike Job. No, Satan challenges *God* to strike Job. God, who declares "the end from the beginning" (Isaiah 46:10), accepts this challenge and gives Satan permission to do it! Wait. So Satan challenged God to strike Job and God gave permission to Satan to strike Job? Yes. So, who or what was responsible for the death of Job's kids? In other words, who or what caused their death? The wind, Satan, or God? All three, but only one was ultimate.

1. The wind caused their death. It really did: "A great wind came across the wilderness and struck the four corners of the house, and it fell upon the young people, and they are dead" (Job 1:19).

2. But Satan caused the wind. We know this because God said to Satan, "All that he has is in your hand" (Job 1:12). The emphasis in this section with all the calamities is that Satan was behind every single one of them. Satan is the epitome of evil, and he does evil because he loves it immensely. Remember, Jesus said, "He was a murderer from the beginning" (John 8:44). God gave Satan enough of a leash to do evil, and he committed murder.

3. But God gave Satan permission to do what Satan wanted to do: "All that he has is in your hand" (Job 1:12). Why would God do this? Satan wanted to inflict suffering upon Job so that Job would curse God to his face (Job 1:11). God knew that. God wanted Job to suffer for reasons that were in line with Job's best interests. God always accomplishes his desires, while Satan only accomplishes his desires when God allows it. And God only allows it when those desires fulfill his ultimate desire. Satan is God's lackey, his pawn, his instrument to do what God wants done. And nothing that Satan does is against his own desire. It's not like God twisted Satan's arm behind his back and threatened, "If you don't strike Job, I'll break your arm." No, striking Job fit perfectly into what Satan already wanted to do.

But let's talk about divine permission for a minute. When I give permission to my boys to do something they want to do, I am using judgment based on my experiences, which are limited and sometimes flawed by a variety of factors. Sometimes I make the wrong decision in giving them permission. I'm not all-knowing or all-powerful. I don't see into the future, and I can't determine the ultimate outcome. There are too many variables I can't account for and can't direct to my liking. I can't and don't plan out the exact details before they occur. God can do all these things. When a being of this ability gives permission, it's different from when we give permission. Would you agree?

When God gives permission for, let's say, wind to strike a house, Satan to inflict damage, a disease to occur, or a person to commit an evil act, his is a planned and purposeful permission.[34] Planned before the world began, and purposeful to bring about his ultimate desire, which for the person of faith is their ultimate good. God gives permission for a tragedy, be it through Satan, a person, a virus, or nature, knowing what outcome it will bring. And if he knows the outcome that his permission will bring, and he has the ability to not grant permission, but decides to grant it anyway, then whatever it is that he is granting is his will, and a type of causality.

The granting of permission is his will, and whatever comes to pass is his will. And the granting of permission and the outcome it brings were planned even before we were born. So God's permission is always one hundred percent aligned with his original intention or will. Nothing takes him by surprise. God's permission is like an *indirect* causing.[35] God means for all of his permissions to accomplish his ultimate aim, which is the ultimate good of the believer, and as A.W. Pink said, "God only permits that for which he has proposed."[36]

So, we have three levels of causality in the death of Job's children: the wind, Satan, and God. But who is ultimately decisive in their death? Who has the final say? God does. The wind and Satan do not have ultimate say. It was God's will for Job's kids to be killed that day by the wind, and by Satan's hand. It really was the wind, and it really was Satan's hand. But the wind and Satan could only move when God gave them permission. Satan's will was to kill Job's children, but his will was not ultimate or decisive. God's will was ultimate and decisive.

The statement of Ephesians 1:11, that God "works all things according to the counsel of his will" is on full display in God's description of Job to Satan following the death of Job's children: "He still holds fast his integrity, although you incited *me* against him to destroy him without reason" (Job 2:3, emphasis mine). Although God didn't do it directly, he holds *himself* responsible for the outcome. Even Job himself attributes the entire sequence of events to God when he says, "The Lord gave, and the Lord has taken away" (Job 1:21). And in case we think Job was incorrect, the narrator of the book confirms Job's assessment of the situation, that Job did not sin or charge God with wrong (Job 1:22). And at the end of the book, after Job was healed, it says, "Then came to him all his brothers and sisters and all who had known him before, and ate bread with him in his house. And they showed him sympathy and comforted him for all the evil that the Lord had brought upon him" (Job 42:11). Again, God's permission is an *indirect* causing.

Loathsome Sores

I will not belabor this for two reasons. One, time and space prohibit it, and two, much of what was said in the section above applies here. After Satan accomplishes his murderous deeds, he goes back to the presence of God. God informs Satan that Job still has not cursed God, despite Job's great loss. Satan then challenges God to attack Job's health, specifically, his "bone and his flesh" (Job 2:5). Again, we see God agree to Satan's challenge, but he gives permission for Satan to do it. In this permission, Satan is still on a leash: He is permitted to attack Job's health but prevented from killing him (Job 2:6).

"So Satan went out from the presence of the Lord and struck Job with loathsome sores from the sole of his foot to the crown of his head" (Job 2:7). Medical doctors and specialists describe what used to be called "Job Syndrome" as autosomal dominant hyper-IgE syndrome (AD-HIES), a rare immune disorder caused by gene mutations, leading to skin and lung infections.[37],[38],[39] It was bad. Consider the following reactions from Job, his wife, and Job's friends:

- Job scraped himself with broken pottery (Job 2:8)

- Job's wife told him to curse God and die (Job 2:9)

- Job's friends didn't recognize him, wept, tore their robes, and sat with him without speaking for seven days (Job 2:12–13)

- Job wished he had never been born (Job 3:11)

- Job wanted to die (Job 3:21)

And all of this was evil. It really was. It was described as such by Job (Job 2:10), Job's friends (Job 2:11), and the narrator of the book (Job 42:11). Yet what or who was ultimately decisive in Job's illness? If modern doctors are correct, as they consider Job's symptoms, it was Job's genes that mutated, leading to infections. So the mutated genes caused Job's illness. But what caused his genes to mutate? We know from the behind-the-scenes conversation that Satan did it, and was therefore causal and responsible. Satan is given power, or allowed to exercise his already-given power, in given situations when God permits it. However, Satan was not ultimately causal, responsible, or decisive in Job's illness. God was. This is how Job and the narrator of the book describe it. When Job's wife tells him to curse God and die, Job says to her, "Shall we receive good from God, and shall we not receive evil?" (Job 2:10). Then the narrator adds, "In all this Job did not sin with his lips" (Job 2:10). Again, at the end of the book when Job's health is restored, the narrator says, "And they showed him sympathy and comforted him for all the evil that the Lord had brought upon him" (Job 42:11).

We need to have a cognitive pathway that accepts that God can allow evil and even send evil without himself being evil. We'll go into depth on this topic in the next chapter. But isn't this what Job meant when he said, "Shall we receive good from God, and shall we not receive evil (from God)?" (Job 1:10, parentheses mine). Isn't this what the narrator meant when he said the Lord brought evil upon Job? No one in the whole book blames Satan, even though we know what happened behind the scenes. The point is, the biblical figures and authors understood that God was ultimately in control of evil that happens, so much so that he is the final, ultimate cause, while at the same time remaining free himself from being evil. Letting this truth sink in, that God has ultimate, decisive control of all evil tragedies, will help us in our emotional healing when we consider that this sovereign God loves us (Romans 8:39), is for us (Romans 8:31), and works all things together for our good (Romans 8:28).

Taking God off the causal hook in tragedy does not help us; rather, it produces more emotional distress, especially anxiety. If God is not the final, ultimate cause for tragedy, then who is? Satan, humankind, nature, or chance? All these options are unpredictable and scary, and at least one of them wants to kill you. I would rather take my chances with God, who loves me and has my best interests in mind. And it's not just that I want to take my chances with God, the Bible confirms it repeatedly: We can rest in the knowledge that neither disease nor disaster happens outside God's will, which is always good and perfect, even when it doesn't seem that way.

A Word of Hope
Knowing the sovereignty of God over disease and disaster helps us in at least three ways. One, we simply don't know how many diseases and disasters God prevents from happening. It is possible that many more would happen if God were not constantly restraining Satan. Two, God can and does heal

diseases and the aftermath of disasters when it pleases him to do so. We can and should pray for this. Three, when it does *not* please God to heal or repair damages, we can respond as Job did because we know that God, not Satan, humankind, nature, or chance, allowed or caused the tragedy for our good. How did Job respond? "Then Job arose and tore his robe and shaved his head and fell on the ground and worshiped" (Job 1:20).

In Job's grief and suffering, he engaged in mournful worship. Job's tearing of his robe and shaving of his head were signs of grief and mourning. There was in Job a tormented mourning and a sincere worship happening at the same time. In his mourning, he worshiped. In his mourning, he was sad, hopeless, and miserable, and in his worship, he let God know about all of it. The humble posture and mindset of worship would eventually cause Job to recognize who God is, and in this recognizing be able to praise God and maybe even thank him for his goodness despite the pain. "Sorrowful, yet always rejoicing" (2 Corinthians 6:10) is how those affected by disease and disaster can live.

Sorrow is normal, right, and good following a tragedy. How much sorrow and for how long depends on the individual. Many tragedies will produce a lifetime of sorrow. Rejoicing following a tragedy is not normal, but it is right and good. And we need to get there in our emotions even if it is mixed with sorrow. Sorrow comes easily. Rejoicing takes a fight. And fight we must. A true, worshipful mind will indeed include rejoicing, even when sorrow is present. This will, at times, take a lot of effort. It's the down-on-your-face, pounding-the-dirt, choking-on-tears times with God that make rejoicing possible. Understanding that heaven awaits us and is present for our lost loved ones who died in Christ, and knowing our Lord's ultimate purpose in our pain, will help us rejoice. And we will smile and come to know the God who is always for us (Romans 8:31), even, or should I say especially, in our most painful times.

Journal Questions

1. How does understanding and really embracing the sovereignty of God over disease and disaster help us emotionally when we experience these tragedies?

2. Psalm 103:3 says that the Lord "heals all your diseases." How can we understand this verse, and how can this verse bring us peace in light of the many diseases around us and the disease that you have or your loved one has right now?

3. Disease and disaster bring real sorrow. Yet the Apostle Paul expected that the early Christians would have a sorrow mixed with rejoicing (2 Corinthians 6:10). How is this possible? How are we supposed to think about tragedy so that we can rejoice along with our sorrow? Do you believe this is possible for you?

4. Get some time alone with God to think about causality. Job did not have a problem with assigning causality to God for the death of his children and his loathsome sores. Yet we have a problem with this. We want to put all the responsibility on physical factors, human decisions, or chance. While physical factors and human decisions are also along the causal chain of tragic events, they are an incomplete way of explaining tragedy. Read Job chapters 1 and 2 and meditate on God's role in tragedy. How does God fit into the causal chain of Job's tragedies? And how, in his role in tragedy, does God remain free of moral responsibility (i.e., free from sin)?

5. Think about your specific tragedy. How does God fit into the causal chain of your tragedy? How can seeing and embracing God's place in this chain help you?

CHAPTER 9

Despicable Evil

When I started graduate school in psychology, I didn't think that I was entering a career where I would daily face the reality of evil. Before deciding on psychology, I thought about being a police officer. After a couple of ride-alongs with officers, I decided it wasn't for me. It was obvious that a career in law enforcement would put me in touch with the reality of evil more than most other careers. But *psychology*? Yes. You may be wondering what I mean by *evil*, or why I am using this word to describe what a therapist deals with in their job. What word would you use to describe the physical, sexual, and emotional abuse of children? Or armed robbery, the sale of illegal drugs to children, assault, active shooter encounters, sex trafficking, domestic violence, racism, and rape? Or what our military veterans have experienced fighting terrorist organizations overseas? Or when a husband leaves his wife and children to fend for themselves because he is no longer "happy"? I call it evil.

Oxford Languages defines *evil* as "profoundly immoral and wicked." My psychology classmates and most of my professors in the early 2000s hated this word. They would never classify any of the acts I described above as evil. Coming from a ministry background, it was hard to wrap my head around their thought process. Child abuse is not *evil*? In my classes, I was surrounded by what is called postmodern thinking, or postmodernism. This is an ideology that regards, or tries to regard, everything as relative. There is no good or bad, right or wrong, virtue or evil. It's all a matter of perspective. "What's right for you is right for you. What's wrong for you is wrong for you. Your truth is your truth and my truth is my truth." In postmodernism, there is no objective standard, or reality, of right and wrong, true and false. I'm sorry, but let's not tell them that their very explanation of objective reality is itself a claim of objective reality.

And if I thought postmodern ideology was bad then, it's worse now. We live in a world that is successfully erasing, or at least changing, the definition of *evil*. We let people get away with murder. Literally. And if you are a politician, anything goes. I'll spare you the rant about this. We know we live in an age that the prophet Isaiah talked about almost 3,000 years ago, of "those who call evil good and good evil, who put darkness for light and light for darkness, who put bitter for sweet and sweet for bitter!" (Isaiah 5:20). And the world will likely continue this way. But those who live by the standard of God's word call good, good and evil, evil. And we won't stop doing this, despite what the world does. Child abuse and the other atrocities I mentioned are evil.

As I spared you a rant in the above paragraph, I'll also spare you from having to read a list of horrendous evils that happen in our world every day. Just turn on the news, or google "today's headlines," and you'll get the list. Instead, we are going to jump right into the focus of the present chapter, which is to examine God's sovereignty over evil, the "profoundly immoral and wicked" acts committed by people against people. I will present to you evidence for the reality that God is sovereign over evil with the conviction that understanding this reality will bring you peace during a time of global uncertainty and turmoil. Additionally, and especially, this understanding will bring you peace in the great uncertainty and turmoil of your own specific evil tragedy. If I can convince you that God is sovereign over the evil that was committed against you personally, that you are in the hands of God and not in the hands of wicked people, Satan, or chance, then you will have peace knowing that the God who loves you also *ordained* (this word explained later) your suffering.

Our Need

The reality of the sovereignty of God over evil is unfortunately not discussed much from the pulpit on Sunday mornings. When was the last time you heard a sermon about it? There may be a variety of reasons for this in our present Christian culture, but it's unfortunate. What other reality can comfort God's people in the present times than knowing that an all-loving

God is also all-powerful? Yes, powerful enough to be sovereign over even the evil acts of humans, so that neither humans nor Satan nor chance are ultimately decisive. That God, "who works all things according to the counsel of his will" (Ephesians 1:11) is not limited by the evil desires of humans or Satan, and that the "all things" includes all tragedies, even evil tragedies committed by people.

Five times in the introduction of his book, *The Sovereignty of God*, written in the early 1900s, Arthur W. Pink asked the following question: "Who is regulating affairs on this earth today—God, or the devil?" He then made the following statements:

> It is in view of what we have briefly referred to above that we say, present-day conditions call loudly for a new examination and new presentation of God's omnipotency, God's sufficiency, God's Sovereignty. From every pulpit in the land it needs to be thundered forth that God still lives, that God still observes, that God still reigns. Faith is now in the crucible, it is being tested by fire, and there is no fixed and sufficient resting place for the heart and mind but in the Throne of God. What is needed now, as never before, is a full, positive, constructive setting forth of the Godhood of God. Drastic diseases call for drastic remedies. People are weary of platitudes and mere generalisations—the call is for something definite and specific. Soothing-syrup may serve for peevish children, but an iron tonic is better suited for adults, and we know of nothing which is more calculated to infuse spiritual vigour into our frames than a scriptural apprehension of the full character of God. It is written, "The people that do know their God shall be strong and do exploits" (Daniel 11:32).[40]

The reality of God's working in our universe in and through the evils of this world is exactly the "iron tonic" we need for the present times. I said in Chapter 7 that *sovereignty* means ultimate, authoritative power over someone or something. It's the total, final, autonomous, and decisive

allow it or restrain it. I mentioned earlier that the solution for our inability to perfectly keep God's commands was the breaking of his command, namely, murder. The murder I have in mind was the murder of God's Son, Jesus Christ. The breaking of this command fit within the larger context of his plan, his will of decree. Is it possible for us to be saved without this event? Christians would agree that it is not possible. So, was the murder of God's Son part of God's will? If so, did he ordain it? I mean, did he purpose (determine, establish, appoint) this evil act to occur? Or did he just permit or react to it, and then afterward work it out for our good? The example of the crucifixion of our Lord will help us answer the question, "Does God ordain sin?"

Does God Ordain Sin?

It appears that God permits evil, or sin, when it fits within his larger purpose. But does God ordain sin? By *ordain*, I mean, does he purpose, or determine, or establish, or appoint it to occur? This question is important for our emotional stability. When evil happens to me directly, believing that God permitted it helps a little. But believing that God ordained it helps immensely. Bare permission means that he is dependent on a person, demon, or circumstance to present a situation where permission from God is needed. Considering God as dependent on anyone or anything to accomplish his purposes weakens his attributes. God is God. He does whatever he pleases (Psalm 115:3, 135:6) needing permission from no one. If we do use the word *permission*, it is a planned permission,[41] and as I said in the last chapter, an indirect causing.[42] It was planned, or indirectly caused, before the world began. God planned to permit something. He orchestrated circumstances so that the something would need his permission. That something was in his full view and control before it happened. Though he does give permission, this word alone doesn't fully describe the sovereign God of the universe "who works all things according to the counsel of his will" (Ephesians 1:11).

To say that God ordains all actions that come to pass presents God as sovereign, which he is, and fits better with the biblical narrative. He is in complete control and declares the end from the beginning (Isaiah 46:10), because he has determined to bring it to pass. He doesn't declare the end from the beginning because he can see the future, like a fortune teller. He can declare the end from the beginning because he ensures that what he wants to happen actually does happen. He decrees and then executes.[43] "My counsel shall stand, and I will accomplish all my purpose" (Isaiah 46:10).

If God ordains an evil act to occur to me directly, I take more comfort from knowing it is from him, that it was his idea, than thinking that the idea came from somewhere else. Put me in the hands of a loving Father rather than in the hands of wild circumstances, unstable humans, or a demon who wants to torture me. Evil hurts, and our emotional stability will be compromised regardless of what we believe. But believing in the fullness of God, the absoluteness of God, the God-ness of God, will help stabilize your emotions in the midst of turmoil.

So then, does God ordain sin? Does God ordain when an evil act occurs? The short answer is yes. But before I explain further, I would like to point out that this does not mean that God is the author of sin. God hates sin, and he would not be the author, or generator of it. Rather, God uses sin, or directs it, to accomplish his purposes. This is what it would mean to say that God governs the whole world. He can govern a world full of sinners by directing their sin to accomplish his goals. That God is not the author of sin, but rather uses the sins of humanity to accomplish his purposes, relieves God of any responsibility for sin, and holds people fully responsible for their actions. As we saw in Chapter 3, wanting to sin is the natural preference of all people. People sin because they *want* to. It is within their preference to. God just directs humanity's sin according to his will of decree, and holds them accountable. "The human mind plans the way, but the Lord directs the steps" (Proverbs 16:9 NRSV).

The King of Assyria

This is clearly seen in Isaiah 10. Through the prophet Isaiah, God pronounced judgment ("woe") on a people (the Assyrians) whom he was going to use as his instrument to punish the Israelites. And then after God used the Assyrians to accomplish his purpose, he would punish the Assyrians for what they did to the Israelites.

Woe to Assyria, the rod of my anger;
>   the staff in their hands is my fury!
Against a godless nation I send him,
>   and against the people of my wrath I command him,
to take spoil and seize plunder,
>   and to tread them down like the mire of the streets.
But he does not so intend,
>   and his heart does not so think;
but it is in his heart to destroy,
>   and to cut off nations not a few. (Isaiah 10:5–8)

When the Lord has finished all his work on Mount Zion and on Jerusalem, he will punish the speech of the arrogant heart of the king of Assyria and the boastful look in his eyes. (Isaiah 10:12)

The arrogant heart of the king of Assyria was set on one thing: destruction. He did not intend to be an instrument to display God's wrath. His evil deeds were prompted by his own evil heart, and he intended destruction. But this evil heart was directed by God, specifically commanded by God to "take spoil and seize plunder, and to tread them down like mire of the streets." Yet God is not morally accountable for the wicked deeds of the Assyrians. On the contrary, God holds the king of Assyria accountable for his, the king's, actions.

Joseph

God's purposes accomplished through the evil intentions of evil men is also found in the story of Joseph. If you recall, Joseph was the favored son of his father, Jacob. His brothers hated Joseph (Genesis 37:4–5, 8) and were jealous of him (Genesis 37:11), so much so that they "conspired against him to kill him" (Genesis 37:18). One of his brothers, Rueben, did not approve of this, and persuaded the brothers to throw Joseph into a pit instead, intending to rescue him. When a group of Ishmaelites were passing by, Joseph's oldest brother, Judah, suggested they sell him to the Ishmaelites instead of killing him. This they did, without Rueben's consent, for twenty shekels of silver. After selling him, they killed an animal, dipped Joseph's robe in it, and gave it to their father. Jacob said, "It is my son's robe. A fierce animal has devoured him. Joseph is without doubt torn to pieces" (Genesis 37:33). Jacob mourned for his son, and "refused to be comforted" (Genesis 37:35).

Now think about this: There are at least six sins committed by Joseph's brothers.

1. They hated Joseph.

2. They were jealous of him.

3. They conspired to kill him.

4. They were greedy.

5. They deceived their father.

6. They were cruel, that is, without remorse and devoid of empathy.

After the Ishmaelites sell Joseph in Egypt, he is falsely accused of raping his master's wife and thrown into prison (Genesis 39:20). After interpreting the dreams of two inmates, he is forgotten about for two years, until Pharaoh has a dream and pulls Joseph out of prison to interpret it, which Joseph does, and Pharaoh makes him second in command in Egypt. Joseph uses his position to acquire, manage, and store enough grain to preserve the lives of the people in Egypt, and eventually his entire family, during a great famine.

This whole story, up until Joseph interprets Pharoah's dream, is screaming with evil. But look how the inspired author of Psalm 105 speaks of these events: "[God] had sent a man ahead of them, Joseph, who was sold as a slave" (Psalm 105:17). According to the psalmist, God "sent" Joseph to Egypt. Not the brothers, but God. And how did God send him? Through the hatred, jealousy, conspiracy to murder, greed, deception, and cruelty of Joseph's brothers. God's sending Joseph included the intentional sinful behavior of people. Joseph also saw the brothers' actions as God sending him:

> "And now do not be distressed or angry with yourselves because you sold me here, for God sent me before you to preserve life. For the famine has been in the land these two years, and there are yet five years in which there will be neither plowing nor harvest. And God sent me before you to preserve for you a remnant on earth, and to keep alive for you many survivors. So it was not you who sent me here, but God." (Genesis 45:5–8a)

Three times, Joseph affirms that God sent him to Egypt. He even says it was not the brothers who sent him, but God. The brothers (human agency) were employed in the sending. In other words, God sent Joseph to Egypt by way of the brothers selling Joseph as a slave. Or God sending Joseph to Egypt *included* the brother's selling him as a slave. God's vehicle in sending was the brother's sin. They were instruments in the hand of God, directed to do his will. Yet the brothers were fully accountable for their actions. By their own admission, they were guilty of evil: "It may be that Joseph will hate us and pay us back for all the evil that we did to him" (Genesis 50:15). No one in this story let the brothers off the hook of accountability for their actions. They intended evil.

Joseph further describes his view of their behavior in Genesis 50:20: "As for you, you meant evil against me, but God meant it for good." Think about this for a minute. The brothers meant evil; God meant good. In the same actions, one meant evil, the other good. The actions were evil. Hatred, jealousy, conspiracy to murder, greed, deception, and cruelty are evil. They meant their evil actions for evil, and God meant their evil actions for good. What evil did they mean their evil actions for? They meant their evil action to gain money for themselves, be rid of Joseph forever, and cause Joseph to suffer, probably to teach him a lesson. What good did God mean their evil actions for? He meant their evil actions for Joseph's good, for the welfare of the people of Egypt and the surrounding nations, and for preserving the Jewish nation. The same actions were meant by the brothers to bring harm and by God to bring blessing.

Interestingly, it doesn't say that the brothers meant it for evil, but God *used* it for good. As if God, seeing that it was happening, used it, or turned it, for good. No, it says that God *meant* it for good. That is, he intended it for that purpose. The Hebrew word *hasab*, here translated "meant," is used over 100 times in the Old Testament and has been translated to English in various ways throughout these passages. Some of the ways it's translated are *account, conceived, count, devise, esteem, imagine, impute, meant, purpose, regard*, and *think*. Put any one of these translations in the place of "meant," and you'll further get the impact this verse is intended to have. God did not react to the sin of the brothers, and then use it. God, purposing from the beginning, meant it. And God, observing the sinful intentions of the brothers, remained free from moral accountability of their intentions and judged them accordingly.

Jesus

A couple of weeks ago, I went out to dinner with some friends to celebrate a birthday. One of the guys mentioned that his wife was planning a weekend retreat by herself to get some personal time with God in a semi-remote area. He then said that his wife, though she wanted to do it, was a little afraid that something could happen to her, since she'd be alone. Like, what if some psycho is out there who finds her? My friend then told us that he told his wife that since she is going away to have a retreat with God, nothing bad will happen to her. He said that there is no way God would let something happen to her since her purpose is to spend some quality time with him, and if something does happen to her when she is there, then "there is no God." I couldn't believe what I was hearing. This is a faithful Christian man. Has he not read the New Testament? If what he said is true, how should we then explain the way John the Baptist, Stephen, James, and Jesus died?

I am truly not down on my Christian brother and friend. Often, the realities of God can escape us if we are not careful, and we need reminders. My point in this section is to show that if God willed the suffering and horrible death of his own Son, then we are not exempt from the possibility of experiencing the same thing in our lifetime. The Bible is so clear on the matter of God's sovereignty over the death of Jesus that little explanation will be needed. As we look at a couple of passages, keep in mind that the death of Jesus was foreordained by God and executed by his workings through the sinful decisions of men, so that God's will was decisive at every turn, while at the same time the wicked intentions of men were carried out. There were men involved in the crucifixion of Jesus, but God's superintending will governed the entire event, so that the men became instruments in the hand of God, while at the same time fully accountable for their actions because they *did what they wanted to do.*

Jesus sacrificed his life so that we could be saved, and this required his suffering at the hands of sinful men. Was his suffering God's will? Isaiah 53:10 says, "Yet it was the will of the Lord to crush him." According to this verse, Jesus was crushed (destroyed, slaughtered, massacred) because it was God's will that he be crushed. Could he have been crushed if it was not God's will? Jesus said earlier in his life that not even a bird can die apart from God's will (Matthew 10:29). Sounds like God's will was for Jesus to die, and not only to die, but to die in this way.

One of the most striking sets of verses on this subject is Acts 4:27–28, which says, "For truly in this city there were gathered together against your holy servant Jesus, whom you anointed, both Herod and Pontius Pilate, along with the Gentiles and the peoples of Israel, to do whatever your hand and your plan had predestined to take place." After Jesus' death and resurrection to heaven, the disciples were in Jerusalem praying for boldness. They said in their prayer to God that in that city two people and two groups of people came together to "do whatever your hand and your plan had predestined to take place." So, whatever was done by Herod, Pontius Pilate, the Gentiles, and the peoples of Israel was done by the predetermined hand and plan of God.

What did they do?

- Herod mocked Jesus.

- Pontius Pilot knowingly condemned an innocent man to death for fear of the Jews and his own reputation.

- The Gentile soldiers mocked, beat, spat upon, and crucified Jesus.

- The peoples of Israel falsely accused Jesus and persuaded Pilot to execute him.

This was all sin, and it was all predetermined by God. The plan of God for Jesus' life, and for our resulting salvation, included the sinful behavior of people. It was said in a similar way by the Apostle Peter two chapters earlier: "This Jesus, delivered up according to the definite plan and foreknowledge of God, you crucified and killed by the hands of lawless men" (Acts 2:23). This was God's definite plan. Yet none of their behaviors are excused. They are all held accountable by God for their actions.

Our Tragedy

At this point, questions about our own evil tragedy may come to mind. "Was it God's will that my daughter was murdered?" "Did God want my wife to be beaten and robbed at gunpoint?" "Was the sexual abuse I experienced as a child part of God's will?" "Did God want my spouse to cheat on me?" If you asked me these questions, I would likely answer you in the following ways.

No, it was not God's will for these evil events to happen to you. Horrible sin was committed against you, and this makes God's heart hurt for you. God is angry and disgusted by the person who did this to you, and they will receive his wrath in this life or after they die if they don't repent. God weeps with you and is sorry this happened to you. Jesus will comfort you in your pain, because he knows what it is like to be sinned against. Hold on to these truths, for there is nothing I have said in this chapter that negates them.

And then, when you were ready (and only when you were ready), I would also tell you that God is sovereign over your evil tragedy. That somehow, this horrible sin fits within his larger purpose for your life. That if you trust him in this way, he will eventually show you how this awful tragedy is working for your good. I would tell you that God hates the sin that was committed against you and ordained it at the same time, and that trying to limit God's power in this will not give you more peace, but less. That falling into the arms of God, all of God, including his sovereign majesty, will get your through this tragedy.

How This Helps Us

How does knowing, or understanding, and believing in the sovereignty of God over evil help us? There are people who believe that evil can't happen to faithful, committed believers, that God's protection means that they will not experience tragedies (e.g., health, financial, evil). I'm sorry, but this is a lie. If we just took the three faithful, committed believers in the New Testament who died during the time the New Testament was being written, namely, John the Baptist, Stephen, and James, we could say that there is precedent for the beheading, stoning, and stabbing of believers by sinful people. That sounds like evil. If we were to add in the Apostle Paul, the list of evils that can befall believers goes on (2 Corinthians 11:23–27). Adding in Jesus, we rest our case. If evil could happen to our Lord, why couldn't it happen to us?

If you believe that God's protection means that you can't or won't have evil happen to you, that is a made-up belief that doesn't fit with the Bible or real-life experience. Believing something that is not backed up in Scripture or reality will most certainly lead to a mistrust in God, major doubt concerning his power to protect you, and maybe even doubt concerning his existence when evil does happen. God's protection does not mean that we won't experience evil. It means that he will protect us in our experience of evil. The next section of this book will go deeper into that point. For now, I'll just say that having a cognitive pathway in your mind that allows for the reality of God's sovereignty over evil, especially to believers, will guard you from the pitfalls of anxiety, depression, and anger when evil tragedy occurs. You'll be able to say with Joseph, "You meant evil against me, but God meant it for good" (Genesis 50:20).

Many of us worry extensively about evil happening to us. It hasn't happened, but we worry about it happening. Resting in the sovereignty of God over evil should give us a certain peace that comes from knowing that nothing can happen apart from his perfect will. Perfect for us, and perfectly planned before our life even began. Even the very choices people make cannot occur apart from the express purposes of God over and through all things. Remember, limiting God from having authority over the choices people make does not give us more peace, but less. When evil tragedy does happen to us specifically, knowing and believing God's sovereignty over it should cause a certain peace that comes from knowing and believing that our loving Father has this whole ordeal in his hands, and that it has happened exactly as he planned, even the evil events. That this happened *for our good*, even if the result is our death, is the reality that we need to come to believe in order to have peace in the middle of tragedy. The next section of this book will help us continue to find peace in suffering as we explore God's good purposes in our tragedies.

Journal Questions

1. How can understanding and believing in the sovereignty of God over evil help you when an evil tragedy has happened to you?

2. Think about and describe how God's will of command and his will of decree were operative in a specific evil that was committed against you.

3. What do you think about the question, "Does God ordain sin?" Is the answer I have provided difficult to accept? How can accepting this answer help you process the evil tragedy that has occurred to you?

4. Think through the sins that were committed against Joseph, and then meditate on Genesis 50:20, "As for you, you meant evil against me, but God meant it for good." Think through how this applies to Joseph. Then think through and write down how it applies to you. For a specific situation in your life, write down the evil that the person, or Satan, meant for you by that evil, and then write down all the good that God meant for you by that evil. I encourage you to memorize Genesis 50:20 and

learn to think about and apply it to your life whenever evil is committed against you.

5. How would our lives be affected if God's plan did not include the sinful choices and actions of people, which led to the suffering and death of his Son? What feelings are evoked in you when you think that God predestined all of it?

Section IV:
Finding Peace in
Our Suffering

CHAPTER 10

God's Plan

As I am writing this, the current war in Ukraine has produced nearly a half million dead bodies and nearly eight million refugees. Over 1,000 people have been kidnapped in Haiti this year, including an American nurse and her daughter last week. War and drought have created a food shortage of catastrophic proportions for the nearly eighteen million people living in Somalia. Right now, there are seven major natural disasters in the US according to FEMA, affecting countless individuals and their families.

Every day someone is murdered, raped, assaulted, robbed, or kidnapped. Every day people get diseases and experience life-altering accidents. Every day someone's loved one dies. Every day there are divorces, layoffs, and financial devastations. And all this is happening in the city you are living in right now, some of it in your neighborhood, and some of it in your family.

Moms get breast cancer and die. American soldiers get beheaded in Afghanistan. Couples have miscarriages. Spouses cheat on each other. Trusted adults sexually abuse the children that trust them. Children are born with disabilities. Stray bullets from drive-by shootings kill innocent people. Buildings fall on people, bridges collapse, and drunk drivers kill people. People live with daily chronic pain. And all of this happens to Christians. I've seen it. How in the world do we make sense of this? How do we reconcile this with a God who is all-powerful and all-loving, who can stop all this from happening, but doesn't? Is all this God's plan? These are questions we will wrestle with in this section.

And in case you think that suffering only happens today, and that the Bible is out of touch with the horrors we currently experience, remember that there were tragedies in the Bible too. The entire world drowned in a flood. That is babies, children, teens, women, men, elderly, and disabled people. In the Bible, there is cannibalism in the form of parents eating their children, and children being thrown into fire by their parents in the worship of false gods. In the Bible, every Egyptian family woke up to their dead firstborn son. In the Bible, children are mauled by bears, men are eaten alive by lions, men's eyes are gouged out, and people are stoned to death. In the Bible, there is murder, rape, and incest. In the Bible, thousands of men, women, and children die by disease and in earthquakes, fires, wind, and war. In the Bible, there is a reference to people being sawn in half as a form of torture. In the Bible, our Savior and the founder of our faith was tortured and executed in the most brutal fashion in all of history.

This Is Not the Garden, and It's Not Supposed to Be

The world we live in, the one God created, is a dark place. But God' plan for the human race, from the beginning, included this darkness. wasn't dark when he made it, but it became dark, and this too was pa of his plan. God did not intend for all of humanity to live in the Gard of Eden forever. His plan was not *messed up* by Adam and Eve when t ate the forbidden fruit. No, God's plan *included* the fall of Adam and which brought sin into the world. God was not confounded or conf when Adam and Eve gave in to Satan's temptation. God's plan didn It was right on track.

God created a perfect world, a world without sin and without su But he did not intend for it to stay that way. He planned for a sin-i world, a world where people hurt one another. A world where thir always work out. Where people don't live forever, and things forever. A world where people do get cancer and are born with disabilities. Where divorce does happen. Where car accidents and tsunamis do occur. In short, a world of tragedy, loss, pai fering. This world of sin and suffering was necessary for sev that we will explore in this chapter and in this section.

As we move through the explanations for why sin and suff the present reality we live in, please keep in mind the overa this book: to find peace when facing tragedy. That is, freedom depression, and anger during and following a tragic experience. Is that not God's goal with every person? That during and following a tragedy, we would see God, life, and tragedy through a particular lens that allows for peace, rather than distress, to occupy our mind? That when tragedy strikes, we would try to see it from God's perspective, and that his perspective would in some way minister to our souls, helping us to emotionally cope and process the tragedy? A major goal of the Bible is that we will learn how to think, see the world, and understand our experiences in light of tragedy, and that in our tragedy, we can still have peace.

That sin and suffering occupy our present reality is undeniable. It's true, real, and we have to live with it. The biblical explanation for why it's is presented in this book because I believe that a proper understanding vill help in our emotional healing. Theology, the study of God and is beliefs, is not supposed to be boring, impractical, or only for elite cs. Good theology should be exciting and practical, and it should minds and hearts of everyone. Theology should be applicable yday lives, including our darkest and most painful moments. logist, and a Christian, my intention is to bring the realities our present sufferings in a way, and with the intention, to ing in and during tragedy, to alleviate painful emotions, lasting peace, hope, and joy.

esented in these chapters on suffering have ministered it hours and are the things I wish I could share with person I speak with in my office. As I said earlier aim to have all the answers to this difficult subject, he final word on it. I have wrestled over the years irtbreaking realities of suffering, in light of an God, and I learn more season by season. The easily, that is, on the surface, suggest that the owerful and all-loving God. It would seem l does exist, given the gruesome reality of t all-powerful or not all-loving. But that e.

tand why and how we live on a sin-, at is getting worse year by year. I've wrestled with this repeatedly in my head as I look at the evidence in my office, on the news, in my community, and in my own life. I hope that you will wrestle with this in your own mind as well and think below the surface with me.

As we now look at evidence from Scripture, let's keep in mind that God did not lose the battle against evil. God and Satan are not equals, duking it out. Nor does God reluctantly acquiesce to the whims and requests of Satan or the decisions and actions of humans because he, God, can't interfere with our free will. On the contrary, suffering, calamity, tragedy, and the sinful human choices that bring about all of this originated in the mind and plan of God long before we even existed.

The Love of God, Redemption, and the Surpassing Beauty of His Grace

The Love of God

What do great movies all have in common? Think about *Titanic, Lord of the Rings, The Last of the Mohicans, Armageddon, Terminator, Marvel Avengers: Endgame, Star Wars,* and *Independence Day*. Each of these had a main character who sacrificed their life for someone they loved. Take *Titanic* for instance. This was the highest grossing film throughout the 1990s. That means this movie made more money than any other movie made in that entire decade. What made a movie about a ship that sank in the Atlantic Ocean over 100 years ago so popular? Arguably, we loved the buildup of Jack's relationship with Rose and him making the ultimate sacrifice of his own life to save her. Or more recently, how about the highest grossing superhero movie of all time, *Marvel Avengers: Endgame*. In the final battle scene, Tony Stark sacrifices his life to save humanity from the powerful Thanos.

I know these are just movies. But they are movies done in such a way that we have a real, emotional reaction to them. Good movies do that. When a movie can make you feel something, the director has done their job, and we should pause to consider it. I think it's human nature to be attracted to stories about love, a kind of deep, passionate, lasting love that leads to the ultimate sacrifice. That's the reason all the heroes died in the movies listed above. They did it for love. Boromir for Merry and Pippin, Duncan for Cora, Obi-Wan for Luke, Leia, Han Solo, and Chewbacca… hopefully you're following. When a hero fights for the love of their life, and then dies or is willing to die for that person, we can't help but be moved.

Ask any boy, and even many men, if they like love stories or romance movies. Most would unequivocally reply, "No," and say something about how those are for girls. Or they might say, "I don't do chick flicks." Lies, lies, lies. Oh, how wrong they are. I have two boys who are very much *boys*, and they would say, "I like action movies, not love movies." Hmmm, every single action movie worth its salt is also a love, or romance, movie. *Braveheart, Gladiator, Saving Private Ryan, Die Hard,* and even *Rambo* (except Part 1) are love stories. You can't miss it. From beginning to end, the hero is fighting for someone they love. So I say to my boys, "Sorry, you guys do like love movies!"

How about the Bible? What genre of book is it? Really, it's a love story. Ultimately, it's a story of God's relentless love for his people. From beginning to end, it's a story of God's fight for the love of his life, his bride, the church. And our Hero makes the ultimate sacrifice for us. That's right, you and me. And this is not a movie. This is my first point: *Suffering exists in this world so that the love of God could be demonstrated to us.* Like the heroes in the movies listed above, and many more I'm sure you can think of, how was their love demonstrated? It was by their sacrifice. Could they have shown their love in a better way? Probably not. That's why I've called it the ultimate sacrifice. What better way can someone show you their love than by laying down their life?

Jesus Christ showed his love for us by laying his life down for us. Jesus said in John 15:13, "Greater love has no one than this, that someone lay down his life for his friends." About this subject, Paul said in Romans 5:8, "But God shows his love for us in that while we were still sinners, Christ died for us." Could the fullness of God's love for us have been shown in any other way? I don't think so. Creating us was not enough. Taking care of us and even blessing us with material and spiritual gifts was not enough. Coming to this earth as a man and providing the world's greatest teachings and display of miracles was not enough. Dying was necessary.

In order for this to happen, Jesus had to enter a world of sin and suffering. In order for Jesus to be put to death on a cross, he needed such a world. If we had a world with no sin and no suffering, Jesus could not have died in the way he did, and the fullest extent of God's love for us would not, could not, be demonstrated. Think about what Jesus went through: the betrayal by Judas, the deception and slander at the mock trial, the mocking from Herod, the cowardice, selfishness, and negligence of Pontius Pilate, the accusations of the people of Israel who shouted, "Crucify him! Crucify him!" and the beating, scourging, and crucifying by the Roman soldiers. None of this could have happened without a world of sin and suffering. And this was planned by God.

Consider Acts 4:27–28, "For truly in this city there were gathered together against your holy servant Jesus, whom you anointed, both Herod and Pontius Pilate, along with the Gentiles and the peoples of Israel, to do whatever your hand and your plan had predestined to take place." Did you catch that? Herod, Pontius Pilate, the Gentiles (the Roman soldiers), and the peoples of Israel all did what they did according to what the hand and plan of God predestined would take place. So God planned a world of sin and suffering so that his Son could enter it and die in order to show his love for us, "For God so loved the world, that he gave his only Son" (John 3:16).

So, the greatest sacrifice the world has ever seen was the greatest act of love the world has ever seen and was caused by the greatest sins people have ever committed. It was brought about by and through sin and suffering. So when you suffer, know that God, in human form, suffered first. And he did it for love. The world, of necessity, was filled with sin and suffering. This was the only way to bring about the greatest act of love, and the greatest redemption, in the history of the world.

Redemption

What are the effects of this great love? In the films mentioned above, the person or persons for whom the hero died was saved from death. Jack died to save Rose from death in *Titanic*. Colonel Sharp died to save his crew members in *Armageddon*. The biblical story is that God created humans who rebelled against their Creator and were separated from him because of their sin, and so deserving of death. God, in his desire for a relationship with his creation, came to earth as a man and lived among them. To settle God's wrath against humankind for their rebellion, that rebellion needed to be punished, and that punishment was death. God, in human form, willingly stepped in and took the punishment for humanity's rebellion, even though he committed no sin. Humans deserved to be killed by their Creator, but that Creator came to earth as a man and took the punishment for them. As a result, those who put their faith in him are saved from the wrath of God.

When I think about my years of willful, deliberate sinning before I became a Christian, my willful, deliberate sins as a Christian, and my unintentional sinful nature that I wake up to every day, I am floored when I think about how all this is washed clean by the blood of Jesus. That he would willingly step in to take the wrath of God for me, when I'm the one who deserves it, blows my mind every time I stop to think about it.

When we were helping our fourteen-year-old son become a Christian, we watched together *The Passion of the Christ* movie released in 2004, directed by Mel Gibson. Many of you have seen it. This movie, more than others I have seen, depicts the gruesome horrors of Christ's execution. The horrific torture endured by Jesus as portrayed in this film is always hard to watch, let alone accept. There are three scenes that continue to replay in my mind: the one where Jesus is scourged, the one where the soldiers have Jesus in a room and are beating him and putting the crown of twisted thorns on his head, and the one where the nail goes through his ankles. What stands out in my mind is not just the unbearable pain this must have caused, but that those abusing him were laughing and carrying on like it was some kind of party, and that he was the only one suffering.

But then I think about how I was like one of those soldiers, laughing and carrying on when the Son of God was dying in my place. I have no problem understanding that if I had been there, I would have been guilty of killing the Son of God. That Jesus took this torture for all these people, all of us, and me specifically, takes my breath away. I don't know of anyone who would willingly take that kind of abuse on purpose for someone else, especially for the people who were causing it. He didn't deserve it, and we don't deserve the redemptive effects of it.

But this really happened. And what are the continual effects of this one great act, which we described above as God's ultimate act of love? The effects of God's great love for us in the death of his Son is that we are saved. In many cases, saved from a destroyed life by continual living in sin. Though in a greater and more definite sense, saved from eternal hell, which the Bible describes as the "second death." Instead of an eternal separation from God in hell, we pass from this life to eternal life with God in heaven. Jesus' death is our redemption. Our redemption was only possible because of the death of God's Son, which required a world of sin and suffering. So God created a world of sin and suffering so that his Son could die, so that we would know God's great love for us, and so that we could be saved.

The salvation that we have required the death of Jesus, which required that Jesus live in a world of sin and suffering, for the world, by its sin, put Jesus to death. This death, and the effects of it, which was our salvation, was planned before the world even began. The world had a beginning. At some point prior to Genesis 1:1, there was no world, and during that time before Genesis 1:1, God made a decision. That decision included creating a world where people would sin, and suffering would occur because of sin. That decision also included coming to this world as a man to die for the sins of his creation and to make salvation available to this creation.

2 Timothy 1:8–9 says:

> Therefore do not be ashamed of the testimony about our Lord, nor of me his prisoner, but share in suffering for the gospel by the power of God, who saved us and called us to a holy calling, not because of our works but because of his own purpose and grace, which he gave us in Christ Jesus before the ages began.

Before the ages began, God gave us grace in Christ Jesus. How could anyone have grace in Christ Jesus? Jesus had to die. No one would have grace without the suffering and death of Christ. So, in order to have a world where God's future creation would receive grace in Christ Jesus, God had to create a world that includes suffering.

Or consider the "book" that is mentioned in Revelation. Revelation 13:8 says, "And all who dwell on earth will worship it, everyone whose name has not been written before the foundation of the world in the book of life of the Lamb who was slain." In the verses prior, the author is describing the power of the beast. Here in verse 8, he says that everyone whose name is not in "the book of life of the Lamb who was slain" will worship this beast. But when was this book written? When were the names of people who will not worship the beast written down? They were written down in this book "before the foundation of the world": before the world began, before anyone was even born.

Think about that. God had a book about Jesus being slain before sin or suffering existed. Conceived in the mind of God before the world began, was a world of suffering that would slay the Lamb. The Lamb couldn't be slain unless he lived in a world of suffering, a world where people are jealous, selfish, fearful, power-hungry, money lovers, liars, and murderers. This is the type of world that God planned before the foundation of the world, in order to have his Son slain in it, in order to offer redemption to us.

The Surpassing Beauty of His Grace

Total Darkness
Imagine living in a world of total darkness, that is, a complete absence of light. You can't even see your hand in front of your face. You can't see faces or objects or even the food that you find to put in your mouth. And you don't know what food, or a mouth, even looks like. And let's say you were born into this. Everyone was. This is different from being blind in a world where other people can see. In this world, no one can see. No one can describe how anything looks. There are no books, televisions, phones, cars, or houses. There could be no meat, because no one would know to kill an animal for food or be able to do it if they did know how. There would be no crops or harvest or grocery stores. Nothing.

Now imagine that somehow in this world, some people survived to adulthood living in complete darkness. Always bumping into everything. Not knowing what they were doing or who they were talking to, but somehow managing to get enough water and food to survive. Somehow getting enough protection from the elements. Somehow not dying from lack of sanitation. And somehow reproducing and making babies.

I know that the world I described would be impossible to survive in. But if it were possible, it would be absolutely miserable. Unending, miserable darkness. There are no schools, work, leisure, travel, or entertainment. No one has ever seen anything, so no one can make meaning of any sounds or experiences. No one can help one another. And no one knows what light looks like. It's never been seen, so the mind can't even comprehend what it is.

Imagine living in this condition into adulthood. You've spent your whole life in total darkness with a few others who have survived, and then one day, you see a beam of light from the sky shining directly down to the earth. The first ever beam of light. You don't know what it is, or what to call it, but you are amazed by it. What do you think you would do? You would go to it, right? Everyone would. I mean, who would not want to go see this amazing thing? One light in the whole world. Since there is no other light, and everything else is darkness, you can see this beam of light for miles. And the light is even more radiant because everything around it is complete darkness. People would travel for miles to see it and get in it, and news would spread about this amazing thing.

And then let's say this light grew to light up a whole city. People would want to stay there, right? They would be fighting to get in and live there. Imagine the possibilities in this new city. It would completely change their lives forever. There would be immense gratitude for this newfound experience. Many would recall the former days when all they knew was darkness. If it were possible, many, I imagine, would even form rescue missions, sending people of the light into faraway dark places to rescue people of the darkness by bringing them into the light. Many from the darkness, I think, would not want to come, maybe for fear of the unknown or unbelief that a world of light actually exists. Or maybe some of them would have grown accustomed to or comfortable in such misery. But those who did come would be eternally grateful, and would wonder why anyone would not accept, and love, the light.

Total Light

Now imagine a world of total light. Very bright light. Everything and everywhere is brightly lit. There is no darkness of any kind, anywhere, ever. No one has ever experienced darkness, so they don't know what it is and can't imagine it. Light is everywhere, and there is no way to create darkness, not even by going indoors or closing window curtains. I know, this is fiction, like the total darkness, but stay with me. In this world of light, there are no words or images to describe darkness. Day or night, it's always light.

Now imagine, after years of everyone living in this light, a beam of light comes down from the sky to the earth. What would happen? Nothing. No one would even see it. They couldn't, because everything around them would be light. This amazing beam from the sky would go unnoticed. And let's say that this beam of light, if they touched it, could somehow change their lives for the better forever. They would miss it. And even if someone, somehow was able to see it, let's say with some special glasses or telescope, and experienced it, and then tried to tell everyone about it and get them to see and experience it, it's likely that no one would believe it or even care. I mean, why would they? They have been living in light their whole lives. They'd say, "What's so special about that beam of light? See, we've got all the light we need right here. The last thing we need is more light." It would be hard to convince them otherwise.

Comparison

What do you think about these two fictional worlds? Do you see that those who lived in darkness were able to find the light when the light came to earth, but those who lived in light could not see the light even when it was shining down from heaven? This is why suffering exists on the earth: so that we can see the surpassing beauty of Christ in a world of total darkness. Otherwise, we'd miss him. Suffering exists so that we, by comparison to the darkness around us, can see the light of Christ, the surpassing beauty of his grace. This grace would not be so attractive to us if we didn't see and experience the horror, evil, and misery around us. The grace of Jesus Christ is magnified when set against the backdrop of this world of suffering.

If suffering did not exist, we would be like those in the story above who missed the light. Christ would come, but we would miss him. Although that is not the world we live in, many still do miss him. Maybe they haven't suffered enough or seen enough misery, or are hardening their hearts to the cold realities of this world. For Christians, we know we live in a world of pain and suffering, and that is what makes the beauty of God's grace look so good to us. We could never find Christ, and we wouldn't even seek him, without suffering. It's the sorrow of this world and in our own lives that makes us see the beauty of God's grace and our need for redemption and healing from this sorrow.

It's in this suffering that we find Christ and are continually grateful for him. But I am getting ahead of myself. In the next chapter we will take a closer look at how and why our personal suffering is necessary for us. For now, we have learned that God planned a world of pain and suffering for very specific reasons. But what does this all have to do with our emotional well-being? *Everything.* Our emotions are challenged when we feel that our suffering has no purpose, no meaning, is arbitrary, or that God is not actually in control. Knowing that we live in a world of planned, purposeful suffering by an all-powerful God who loves us, who did all this for us, and who also suffered with us himself, should give us some measure of comfort in our distress and make us pause to consider the bigger picture. Let's continue to work this out in our minds as we consider more specifically how God uses suffering for our good.

Journal Questions

1. I said in this chapter that suffering exists in this world so that the love of God can be demonstrated to us. How was his love demonstrated to us? How important is it that we understand God's love for us? How can understanding God's love for us help us in our suffering?

2. I described how the suffering of Jesus Christ was part of God's plan all along. Read Acts 4:27–28 and think about the various players in God's plan: Herod, Pontious Pilate, the Gentiles, and

the peoples of Israel. How was each person a part of God's plan? It says that they did whatever God's hand and plan had predestined to take place. Can understanding the suffering and death of Jesus in this way help you in your season of suffering? If so, how?

3. One of the effects of God's great love for us is our salvation, or redemption, from sin and hell. This can be described as God's grace. Was the love of God and his grace to us possible without a world of sin and suffering? What do you think about 2 Timothy 1:8–9 and Revelation 13:8? If it is challenging to accept that God planned a world with sin and suffering before the world began in order to eventually show his love for us and demonstrate his grace, how can you overcome that challenge? How can you accept God's wise and perfect plan in light of your personal suffering?

4. Think about what it would be like to live in total darkness and in total light. Which world would make it possible to see the perfect light of Jesus Christ? Remember that it's not just that God gives grace, but that his grace is beautiful, and that we can best see and appreciate beauty when it's compared to something ugly. How does the sin and suffering of this world compare to God's grace? Describe how living in a world of sin and suffering helps us see the beauty of God's grace. Describe how in your specific suffering, you are able to better see and appreciate the beauty of God's grace.

5. The bigger picture of God's plan for this world includes sin and suffering. I say *bigger picture* because in our own suffering, it's not just about us. The suffering that we experience fits into a larger context that is all part of the perfect plan of God. How does, or how could, thinking about the bigger picture help you in your suffering?

CHAPTER 11
Of Necessity

Becoming a psychologist, I had the privilege of working as an intern with children in two difficult clinics for a total of 2,000 hours. One was a domestic violence shelter for abused women and their children. The other was a county facility for mental health and substance abuse. The former operated on donations, and the latter on tax dollars. The children there had experienced physical and emotional abuse, violence, divorce or separation, mental health challenges, substance abuse, and poverty. The perfect job for an unpaid and inexperienced intern! I said it was a privilege, and I really meant that. Yes, I was unpaid and inexperienced, not to mention overworked and underappreciated, but the exposure I had to real life was worth more than pay. And this came to me before I had children of my own.

The biggest problem with the children was not really the issues I mentioned. The problem was the almost complete lack of parenting many of them had received. Not all, but many, had never received a reprimand, let alone a time out or loss of privileges. For those that did receive reprimands, it was from an out-of-control parent yelling at them. Imagine raising a child with only harsh correction, and no accountability, training, or appropriate discipline. What do you think your child would become? You don't have to guess. I'll tell you what many of the children at the clinics were like. They were out of control, some of them completely. They displayed some of the most inappropriate, self-destructive, and cruel acts toward others you can think of. I'll spare the details for lack of space in this chapter, but use your imagination, and then bow your head in relief and offer a prayer of gratitude if this is not what your child is like.

It would be hard to blame these children for their behavior. They just didn't have the parenting they needed. Unfortunately, most of them are likely now, at best, repeating the same lack of parenting with their own children, or they are in poverty, or worse, in prison for a crime. It's likely that both clinics are still very full, and the interns there now are having the same experiences I did.

The simple takeaway from this experience is that an uncorrected child does inappropriate things. Or, that a spoiled child doesn't play nicely with others. That's the most nonclinical way to say it. Yes, many of them were ᴠoiled. Spoiled with the freedom to do whatever they wanted with few ᴨo consequences, or an overly demanding parent they were afraid of. ᴇr way, many of these children were alone, trying to figure out how to ᴧng in the world without a healthy parent to help them. And left to ᴠves, they went astray, and some ended up at the other place where ᴨterns worked: juvenile hall, or juvie, as we called it. That's soci-ᴧse to behavior gone awry: prison. If your parents don't parent will.

ʹ, not everyone who is unparented or parented poorly ends up ᴧl know or have heard of people who have turned their lives horrible upbringing. There are probably more of these ᴧn count. Maybe for some of you, that's your story. I'm messing up in your parenting, being overly permissive ᴧin your kids. My wife and I have been on both sides ur kids are not ruined. The point of this story is ᴧhat correction, or call it training or discipline, is the absence of it is very bad. Try to think of any ᴨ, training, or discipline is not applied and it ᴠould be one broke, uneducated, overweight, ʹrection, training, and discipline were not ᴧat's what we are." And you may be right. ᴧven worse off without the correction, ᴠe had. It's not optional; it's required.

From Parenting to God

I was a kid in the '80s. I'm grateful that back then leather belts were used for more than holding up your pants, wooden spoons for more than stirring pasta, and ping-pong paddles for more than playing ping-pong! Seriously. My behind didn't appreciate it at the time, but my soul is forever grateful! I shudder to think how I would have turned out if it weren't for good old-fashioned, "take you out to the woodshed" discipline. I was disciplined, and I still got caught up in many of the "big" sins, so imagine what would have happened if I had not been disciplined. Now, I don't at all advocate for physical abuse. Spanking can be, and is, done incorrectly and abusively all the time, and that is unacceptable. But corporal punishment at certain ages in the form of spanking only, done correctly, using a calm, controlled, and measured method only, is not abusive. Quite the contrary. Letting your child go astray without correction may be the real abuse.

If you grew up in a stable Christian home, it is possible that you have avoided many sins like sexual immorality, theft, drunkenness, and cruel violence, but I doubt that you have been able to completely curb your pride, deceit, fear, lust, selfishness, and self-pity. And if so, it may be easy to judge those who, like me, have committed those other sins, along with sins of the heart. But the sins of the heart are just as bad and just as deadly. What was it, and what is it, that continually gets these sins out of our life and shapes us into the person God means us to be?

Like the children in the clinics, we need a parent who can apply wise, calculated, restorative correction to our lives. Even if you had a parent who won the Parent of the Year award for awesomeness, that person was not able to fulfill the role of Father that only God can. Parents have a God-designed purpose in a child's life for correction and character training. But that only goes so far and for so long. Consider what the author of Hebrews says about the topic of discipline as it applies to our life, to a parent's role, and to God:

> And have you forgotten the exhortation that addresses you as sons?
>
> > "My son, do not regard lightly the discipline of the Lord,

> nor be weary when reproved by him.
> For the Lord disciplines the one he loves,
> and chastises every son whom he receives."

It is for discipline that you have to endure. God is treating you as sons. For what son is there whom his father does not discipline? If you are left without discipline, in which all have participated, then you are illegitimate children and not sons. Besides this, we have had earthly fathers who disciplined us and we respected them. Shall we not much more be subject to the Father of spirits and live? For they disciplined us for a short time as it seemed best to them, but he disciplines us for our good, that we may share his holiness. For the moment, all discipline seems painful rather than pleasant, but later it yields the peaceful fruit of righteousness to those who have been trained by it. (Hebrews 12:5–11)

This section in Hebrews does not imply that discipline used by God is punitive, but rather, it is restorative or productive. It's a constructive use of discipline with the intent of producing something better than what was before. Like a father disciplines his son to train his character in a particular way, God disciplines us to train our character in a certain way. When my sons are lazy, deceitful, or mean to others, my discipline is not so they will "learn their lesson." It's for the purpose of creating in them the opposite of what they are without my intervention. It's turning children prone to laziness, deceit, and cruelty into hardworking, honest, and loving men—men who will be able to take care of their families, love God, and benefit society. When God disciplines us, he has a *prescriptive* intention.

God's discipline is designed for us, for our good. The process is painful but purposeful. What would we be without it? God knows, and in his all-knowing wisdom, judges the thing left undisciplined as worse off than if disciplined. So he gives us what we need. Often, we ask for changes in our life that only discipline can accomplish. Have you ever asked God to make you more loving? Maybe he sends someone into your life who hates you and is evil toward you in order to make you more loving. Have you ever asked God to increase your faith or make you more courageous? Maybe God puts challenges in your life to help in these areas. Or how about to be humbler? That's a scary prayer. It might be safer to humble ourselves than to ask God to do it! Seriously, though, how do we think we are going to grow in our humility, I mean really become a humble person, if not through being humbled?

God is constantly at work in our lives, shaping us into who he wants us to be. And that shaping is often painful. Of course it is! Changing bad habits and character weakness is not easy, and so we fight against it. Fighting against God in this way is like a block of wood or clay fighting against a sculptor saying, "Don't make me into something more beautiful or useful. I want to continue to be a block of boring, useless material!" It doesn't make sense, right? But we have learned our whole lives to avoid hardship. And when it happens, we are shocked and often angry. But hardship, or suffering, is a necessary part of life if we ever intend to be better than we are.

Two Diets

The Western Diet

I'm a Westerner who grew up on the Super-Size meal from McDonalds, Jumbo Jacks from Jack-in-the-Box, and 59-cent bean and cheese burritos from Taco Bell. And when I wasn't in fast-food drive-throughs, I was snacking on Doritos, Snickers, and Skittles. I don't think we ever read food labels in the '80s! Red Dye 40, how harmful could that be? High-fructose corn syrup, no problem. I guess we have learned a lot since then, because now there are healthy alternatives, or at least now we care about the other options. Think gluten-free, dairy-free, dye-free, and all-natural ingredients. This is probably a good change for us. But the Western (American) diet is something we all know all too well. We have grown accustomed to a processed, prepackaged, high-fat, high-calorie, high-sugar, large-quantity diet. Whether this describes your diet or not, statistically, this has been to our detriment, as the US is the most obese high-income country in the world.

But this book is not about food. There is another diet we have grown accustomed to in North America: the diet of *comfortability*. In the US, right now we have got to be the most comfortable generation in the most comfortable place in the entire history of the world. Do we have crime? Yes. Do we have disease? Yes. Are there streets and even towns in this country that are like the pit of hell? Sure. And is there a chance that our nation could implode on itself from political and racial division? Yes. And is there a chance that while we are fighting each other, our enemies overseas could launch an attack? Absolutely.

But by and large, our neighborhoods are safe. We can walk our dogs mostly without fear of robbery, kidnapping, or rape. By and large, we have medical care. We have vaccinations, medications, and hospitals. By and large, our police are not corrupt, extracting money from citizens with a threat to "pay me or I'll put you in jail." By and large, our country is not war torn. By and large, people are not starving. I understand that I say all this, and there are people right here who can't leave their house for fear of crime, who have been abused by a police officer, who can't access medical care, who live in a place that has been shot up, and who are starving. I get it. But as I said, by and large, this does not represent the whole by comparison to many other places on earth.

What is more representative of the whole is that we, as a nation, have it pretty easy by comparison. Our middle class, which makes up around 50 percent of the country, live better than most people in the world. And the US poor are not like the poor in developing countries. Many people become poor and homeless here due to unwise choices, substance abuse, and mental illness, and are scattered within the general population. It's common in other countries to find entire regions of poor and homeless people, people who are born into poverty who will never escape it.

I'm not complaining about the comfortability that we enjoy here. I'm just acknowledging it. I'm a consumer of the American dream. My paternal great-grandfather came here from Italy and started a shoe business that was carried on by my grandfather, and then my dad. My maternal grandfather came here from Italy and started a fishing business. My mom and dad were business owners. I decided to go to college to work as a pastor, and then back to college to become a psychologist. We all pursued our dreams. Many of us enjoy freedom of choice when it comes to education, employment, place of residence, and lifestyle.

In our lifetime, we have seen a revolutionized technological system that, in many ways, has made our lives easier. We enjoy cell phones, the internet, GPS, Uber, Netflix, Spotify, Amazon, Instagram, electric cars, and an endless variety of apps. We enjoy limitless options for recreation and sporting opportunities, to play or just watch. We enjoy boating, good wine, restaurants, tons of food, nice cars, reliable plumbing and electricity, air conditioning, heat, and medical care. I mean, imagine having to walk to get water from a well, light a fire to get warm, grow or kill food, and build shelter with no power tools. Go to a store, a mall, a shopping center, Amazon, or just look in your pantry and see the options to meet every single need and desire we have, and some we didn't even know we had.

It's like we can essentially do anything and go anywhere we want, only limited by how much money we have. And we have really bought in to the idea that life is mostly about money, fun, and relaxation. Have as much fun as possible, make as much money as possible, take as many vacations as possible, and retire as soon as possible. And in retirement, take up fishing, travel the world, and take life as easy as possible. Yet none of what I am saying in this section about comfortability negates anything in prior chapters about suffering. Any of us or our children could develop cancer, become disabled in a car accident, lose our home in a natural disaster, or become a victim of the most heinous sin or crime.

But even with all the suffering in the world, or maybe *because* of it, many of us have made comfortability a kind of religion. When we sacrifice for and prioritize comfortability, seeking it and honoring it above all else, we become worshipers of it. And this "religion" has crept its way into the church. For decades, the church has worshiped comfortability and has even created doctrines based on it. Easy believism and the prosperity gospel are as popular as they are among evangelicals because comfortability is so prioritized for today's Christian. Many Christians today believe God expects nothing from them and wants everything for them. And if you're not healthy, wealthy, and prosperous, well, you must be doing something wrong.

God's Diet

Comfortability may be the preferred Western diet, and it may be the diet of many churches in America, but it's not *God's* diet. The Bible teaches a much different one. The founder of our movement was falsely accused and condemned to die on a Roman cross. And he said, "If anyone would come after me, let him deny himself and take up his cross daily and follow me" (Luke 9:23). This doesn't sound like it's going to be comfortable. Jesus also said, "If the world hates you, know that it has hated me before it hated you" (John 15:18) and "In the world you will have tribulation" (John 16:33).

Jesus was born to a poor couple in a stable with farm animals. After his birth, his parents fled with him to Egypt to avoid his being murdered by Herod. Talk about an unstable early childhood experience! Jesus' dad presumably died before Jesus was thirty, and Jesus took on the family business. When Jesus started his ministry at age thirty, he left his home and was an itinerant preacher, while he and his followers lived off minimal resources, and he had "nowhere to lay his head" (Matthew 8:20). He was frequently persecuted, avoided certain areas, and his life was threatened repeatedly. This culminated in his arrest, torture, and crucifixion by the Romans. And we are called to *follow* him. So much for easy believism and the prosperity gospel!

Because we walk as light in a world of darkness, the Christian life is hard. Jesus has called us to make disciples (Matthew 28:19) in a world hostile to Christianity. He has called us to live holy (1 Peter 1:15) in an unholy world. And the more we try to make disciples and live holy in hostile territory, the harder life will be. But choosing comfort in this life could mean forfeiting it in the next (Luke 9:24–25). So we need to be careful what we choose. Living a life committed to Christ may mean that you will suffer.

The first Bible I ever owned, and actually read, is now sitting in my closet. It's the Bible I used as a young Christian, when I was a young man in my early twenties. It now has no cover, the spine is in four pieces, and there are several loose, torn, and freestanding pages. It's basically a stack of tattered paper beyond repair. It's marked up in various places from cover to cover with underlines, highlighted verses, and chicken-scratch notes in the margins. There are still grains of sand in it from reading it on the beaches of California. It smells of ocean air and is stained with tears of affliction.

The Bible has helped me as I have wrestled through tragedies in my life, and it has especially helped with the question many of us ask when facing hardship. The question goes something like this: "Is there meaning in my suffering?" or "What is the purpose of my suffering?" When tragedy strikes, the human mind wants to know *why*. One of my favorite books is *Man's Search for Meaning*,[44] by Viktor Frankl, a Jewish psychiatrist who survived several years in Nazi death and concentration camps. The book is a retelling of his experiences. The emphasis of the book is on the importance of finding meaning in our sufferings. The suffering he and his fellow Jews experienced was severe, beyond most of our imaginations. Frankl described how meaning in their suffering was all they had when everything else was taken from them, and how meaning was necessary for survival. He often quoted Friedrich Nietzsche, who appropriately said, "He who has a why to live for can bear almost any how." How true.

I think that there is meaning in our suffering, and that God has meaning for us in our suffering. Think about it. If God is not a sadist (someone who inflicts pain for the sheer pleasure of it), and if God is not too weak to stop the sufferings of his creation, yet causes or permits suffering, he must have a good reason for it. However, we should be careful to not use *our* definition of what is good to judge what God does. When something tragic happens to us or we see something tragic happening in the world, our first thought may be to say, "That's not good" or "not right," or "not fair." When we do this, we are playing divine referee on God's playing field. He is the judge of what is good and right and fair, and his is the only opinion that ultimately matters. Our definition of good, right, and fair is flawed and subject to our experiences, thoughts, beliefs, and culture. God's opinion and actions are always good, right, and fair. Something that is tragic and looks "not good" may be very good to God.

For the rest of this chapter, we will consider God's meaning, or purpose, in and for our suffering. That is, what his intentions may be for the suffering that has occurred in your life. Understanding that there is real meaning behind your suffering will hopefully help alleviate some of the emotional pain you are experiencing due to it. Please understand that this is only a summary of God's meaning in our suffering. Whole books have been written about this subject (e.g., *The Problem of Pain*, by C. S. Lewis[45]). What follows aligns with the idea that how we think about our tragedy will affect how we feel. If you believe your tragedy, your suffering, is meaningless or that no good could possibly come out of it, that is a recipe for depression, anxiety, and anger. On the other hand, emotional healing comes from the understanding that your tragedy or suffering is meaningful and that good can come from it. I think that is God's overarching message to us in the Bible about suffering.

Repentance

God wants a relationship with you. A *real* relationship. He wants to be your God, your Father, your Lord, and your friend. He wants real intimacy. Because of this, let's assume that blessings and sufferings are placed so that you will have a relationship with him. Blessings should cause us to praise, glorify, and appreciate God. Sufferings should do the same, but also cause us to see our need for God, running to him from any sin we have in our life. God is holy, and his people must be holy in order to have a relationship with him. This is a big deal. So big that one sin, one act of unholiness, separated the first man and woman from God in the Garden of Eden. Think of what a lifetime of unrepented sin will do.

The Greek word for *repent* is *metanoeō*, which means to change one's mind. Repentance is a turning of one's mind, which would turn one's desires, or at least one's behaviors, away from something toward something else. When life is comfortable, and let's say it's because we've received lots of blessings (e.g., in finances, good health, satisfaction in work, and quality relationships), there may be nothing in our life that would cause us to question the path we're on. If it ain't broke, don't fix it, right? Comfortable people often don't see their need for change. They have all they want and need.

But take all that away. Cause loss and pain to come into that person's life. Make them uncomfortable. Hardship and tragedy will often cause someone to see their need for God. In our desperation we may cry out to God for help. Depending on the tragedy, we may see the brevity of life, understand our own mortality, and realize our limitations and frailty.

Have you ever seen someone turn to God without seeing life in this way? In twenty-five years as a Christian, I've had the opportunity of seeing several people turn from a life of sin to God, and I've never seen someone repent who's comfortable. When someone repents, it's usually because of a difficulty in their life that makes them start to see life differently.

From cover to cover, the Bible shows God using suffering in people's lives to move them to repent from their sin and turn to him. It doesn't always work out that way. It didn't then, and it doesn't now. There are thousands, maybe millions, of people who suffer every day and with no repentance. But there are many whose suffering has turned them to repentance. Psalm 119:67 says, "Before I was afflicted I went astray, but now I keep your word." Affliction, in this sense, is restorative. This is not to say that suffering is never punitive. God *is* shown in the Bible to use calamity as punishment for sin. How do you know which it is for you? Is your suffering restorative or punitive? I would say that if you are even asking that question, then for you it is likely restorative. For you, the suffering is probably intended as a wakeup call to repent.

Sanctification

A secondary reason, at least for Christian suffering, is our sanctification. Our sanctification refers to the transformative process by which we are made holy, or purified, or set apart, for God's special work or purpose. In the Christian life, repentance is like cleaning up a filthy dog so it can come into the house. Sanctification is making the dog actually useful for something. Repentance is where God starts with us, but it's not the end.

There are many real-life analogies that are helpful for understanding the biblical realities of suffering for sanctification. Gold is placed in the fire to remove its impurities. A block of stone is cut and chiseled into a beautiful statue. A dilapidated building is destroyed and rebuilt into a new and better one. Weak muscles are broken down to build stronger ones. Cancer is cut out by a surgeon. A wild horse must be broken before it is of any use. In virtually every area of life, we are willing to accept that struggle, suffering, or difficulty is required for growth and improvement. The saying, "No pain, no gain," is right. Are we willing to accept this in our spiritual life?

God uses suffering to shape us into the people he wants us to be. This teaching is found throughout the Bible. James and Paul state this in very plain language:

> Count it all joy, my brothers, when you meet trials of various kinds, for you know that the testing of your faith produces steadfastness. And let steadfastness have its full effect, that you may be perfect and complete, lacking in nothing. (James 1:2–4)

> Not only that, but we rejoice in our sufferings, knowing that suffering produces endurance, and endurance produces character, and character produces hope, and hope does not put us to shame. (Romans 5:3–5a)

These men saw trials and sufferings as good for the Christian. Trials and suffering can take many forms. Whatever you are facing, know that God is doing something in your life to refine who you are. It's not pleasant, but it is refining you into who God wants you to be. In God's infinite wisdom, he has determined that the particular trial and suffering you are going through is necessary for your spiritual development. He's given you what you need. Like the parented child we described earlier, it's not always what the child wants. But in the end, when the child sees the bigger picture, they appreciate the loving hand of the parent who trained them.

Glorification

Suffering can lead us to repentance, sanctification, and finally, glorification. *Glorification* is a word used in Christianity to describe the final stage of redemption for the believer. It describes our eternal nature in heaven when God has removed the sin nature from our lives after we die. It's the grand finale of sanctification, where God's glory (his praise, majesty, honor, and holiness) is realized *in us*. This is what we look forward to most as Christians. Paul considered it far better for him to depart and be with Christ than to stick around here (Philippians 1:23–24).

Regarding suffering, Paul said, "I consider that the sufferings of this present time are not worth comparing with the glory that is to be revealed to us" (Romans 8:18). God wants us to look at the world around us, with all its glamour, pomp, and comforts, and see heaven, that is, being with Jesus forever in our transformed, sinless nature, and view it as infinitely greater by comparison. Comfortable people will have a hard time doing this. Why would I see heaven as infinitely greater by comparison to this world when I am living my best life now? Sometimes God allows suffering in our life so that we will change our price tags. The world holds great value when things are going well, and heaven is kind of *meh*. When things aren't going great here, the value of here goes down and we see heaven as the greater reward.

Suffering is for our good because it changes our perspective. We begin to live to our fullest potential in Christ when we see that our kingdom is not of this world (John 18:36). Living like a king here has the potential of causing us to make our kingdom here, although it's not. We should be living for the greater kingdom. A life of suffering causes us to long for the heavenly reality that awaits us and to put our hope in what is to come, rather than what is here.

The Western diet of comfortability simply does not have the capacity to bring repentance, sanctification, and glorification in the Christian life. Only God's diet of suffering does. God uses suffering in the life of the Christian to bring about these changes. In the final chapter of this book, we will consider how our purpose in life, as believers, creates a mindset that weathers the storm of adversity. As we see how the right mindset toward purposeful living allows us to accept and even embrace suffering as part of the journey, we will be better positioned to experience peace in the face of inevitable tragedy.

Journal Questions

1. What do you think about the necessity of discipline in everyday life? Could you be where you are today without it? How has your lack of it in any areas affected you?

2. I said, "When God disciplines us, he has a prescriptive intention." What does this mean? In what ways has God disciplined you, and what has been the effect of his discipline?

3. How has the Western diet of comfortability affected our thinking when it comes to correction, training, and discipline?

4. Read and meditate on Luke 9:23, John 15:18, and John 16:33. I used the analogy of diets to help us understand the difference between what the world feeds us and what God is trying to feed us. How does God's diet compare to the Western diet? Do you agree with this comparison? In what ways, if any, have you been rejecting God's diet and embracing the Western diet? How can you begin embracing God's diet more in your life? What effect do you think that will have on your life?

5. I said that God has meaning, or purpose, in your suffering, and proposed three purposes for suffering: repentance, sanctification, and glorification. Do you find that repentance, sanctification, or glorification have been God's purpose in your suffering? If so, how? Has God had other purposes in your suffering? If so, what? How does thinking about meaning, or purpose, in suffering affect how you feel?

CHAPTER 12

Our Destination

"**N**o, we didn't see any movie stars." That's the answer I give to the question I get when I tell people I've been to Hollywood. I hate to burst your bubble, but it's really not what you think. It's kind of dirty, there are lots of homeless people, and there's crime. The median household income is around $50K. That may sound like a lot where you are from, but in SoCal, it's not too much above the poverty line. If you walk down the streets in Hollywood, I guess it feels like any other inner city. Why is there so much idealization over this well-known, historic city? Well, this is where movies are made. Or at least where they got started, right? And it used to be the case that if you wanted to be a movie star, you had to go to Hollywood. Hollywood has a rich history as the birthplace of modern cinematic show business.

And of course, it wouldn't be Hollywood without the iconic Hollywood Sign, situated on Mount Lee, in the Santa Monica Mountains. The Hollywood Sign was erected in 1923, stands at 45 feet tall, and is 350 feet long. It has been featured in hundreds of movies, films, and advertisements. It has become culturally and symbolically known for glamour and stardom. And if you grew up in LA, you must see it in person at least once. And, if you're really crazy, you hike to the top of Mount Lee on your anniversary.

This was where I took my wife for our thirteenth wedding anniversary. Pretty romantic, right? In July 2016, my wife and I planned to hike 6.4 miles through the Santa Monica Mountains to the Hollywood Sign. Why? Because it's cool! And to say we did it. Ok, so the full plan was to hike to the Hollywood Sign, then shower up and get ready at an LA Fitness gym in the area, and then go to a restaurant in Beverly Hills called The Stinking Rose. How's that for romantic?

I remember heading out on the trailhead that warm July morning. We had our minds set on the destination. And it certainly wasn't just about getting there, it was about enjoying the journey and being together. It was a goal we were accomplishing together, which made it even more exciting. As we made it to the top and saw up close this iconic sign that you see in movies your whole life, we felt accomplished and exhilarated. Not just because of the sign. It *is* just a sign. But because we reached our goal, and we did it together.

I use this story to illustrate the idea of destination. *Destination* is an interesting word. If you said *destination* in the 1600s, you would have meant, "the purpose for which anything is intended or appointed." In that sense, our destination would have been the hike itself, not necessarily the finish line. And what was the hike itself? Or what was the purpose of the hike? It was to enjoy time together, celebrate thirteen years of marriage, get exercise, fresh air, and sunlight, and do something we've never done before that sounded interesting and was challenging. That was the purpose of our hike. That was our destination. Word meanings change over time, so when you use the word *destination* today, you typically mean the place itself. In this sense, the Hollywood Sign was our destination.

The Bible describes our destination as believers in both ways. Our destination is both the purpose for which we are intended, *and* the place where we are going—the finish line, if you could call it that. But why is this important? Why should we care about our destination as Christians?

First, God in his infinite wisdom apparently considers it important that we know what our destination is, since he has told us in his word repeatedly. Understanding our destination tells us how to live, what is important, what we should be doing here on earth during the short time we have, and why we do all that we do as Christians. Second, we need to know where we are headed to make sure we end up in the right place. Heading out on that July morning, I made sure to know which direction to take, or we would have ended up lost somewhere in the Santa Monica Mountains. Not the worst place in the world to be lost, but lost nonetheless, and most certainly not reaching the Hollywood Sign. And, finally, no amount of suffering will be unbearable when we understand, and embrace, our God-appointed destination.

As I said, our destination as believers is both the purpose for which we are intended and the place where we are going. So, what is our purpose, and where are we going? I think the answer to this question was best synthesized in the 1600s by English and Scottish theologians in the Westminster Shorter Catechism.[46] Instead of *destination*, or *purpose*, they called it "the chief end of man." They specifically state that, "Man's chief end is to glorify God, and enjoy him forever." That's it. The point of humankind, the purpose for which human beings were created, is to glorify God and enjoy him forever. This is both our purpose for which we are intended, or appointed, and the place where we are going. To glorify God and enjoy him forever is the destination of every believer.

A Life Well Lived

One of the first men of God to have an impact on my life was a man named Kevin. Kevin was the senior pastor of the church I was a part of in my early twenties and then later in my thirties. I had the opportunity to live with him and his family for two years before getting married. Kevin was a man who lived his life completely sold out for the kingdom of God and the gospel of Jesus Christ. To me, he was like a modern-day Apostle Paul. What would the Apostle Paul look like in the twenty-first century? That was Kevin. Kevin didn't lead a church *because* he was the senior pastor. He was the senior pastor because he led the church. I mean, Kevin would have pastored even if he wasn't on the church's payroll. It wasn't just his job; it was his lifestyle.

And what did his lifestyle look like? Before the sun rose every day, Kevin was at a local Starbucks reading his Bible and a Christian book, and writing. This was followed by at least an hour of prayer outside or in his car, while it was still dark. Kevin prayed for every single person in his ministry by name, whether he knew them or not. While living with Kevin, I got into a bad habit of oversleeping. When Kevin noticed this problem, he sat down with me and said, "I've shown my children their whole lives that a man of God gets up early every day and spends time with Jesus before work, and you are not going to ruin this for me." I didn't oversleep anymore after that conversation.

Kevin's first appointment was around 7:00am, usually at a Starbucks. Then he drove around to various places, usually other Starbucks locations, throughout the day to meet with other people in his ministry and people he was trying to help convert. Kevin wasn't a pastor who spent all day in his office. He spent his time with people. From morning till evening, he ministered to people. As a young man, I was intrigued by his lifestyle. Kevin was unlike many of the men I knew. Selfish ambition, the love of money, and pride characterized many of the men around me, even men in the church. These are certainly sins I struggle with all the time. Kevin was different. It was like these sins didn't even cross his mind.

One day in February 2017, Kevin had a heart attack while playing pickle ball at a men's retreat. He was rushed to the hospital, where he lay in a coma. Each evening for that entire week, hundreds of friends, family, and church members gathered at the hospital to pray for Kevin in the parking lot. Countless people flew in from out of town to be with him and his family during this difficult time. For several days, we walked around the hospital building praying for Kevin. One night we did this seven times, like Joshua and the Israelite army walked around Jericho before the walls of the city fell (Joshua 6). Imagine the scene: hundreds of people walking in a parking lot around a hospital building seven times while praying for a single patient inside. But the walls of Kevin's coma did not fall; he did not recover. The heart attack had caused irreversible brain damage, and Kevin died.

His funeral was held on my birthday. Kevin's son gave the eulogy and talked about his father's complete devotion to God, and how he didn't waste his life on frivolous pursuits that ultimately amount to nothing. I don't remember a lot of what he said, except one line: "My dad didn't care about money." Imagine a life where you didn't care about money. Like, you don't even really think about it. I thought about how effective for Jesus we all could be if we didn't think about money so much. That's not to say we shouldn't make money. Missionaries couldn't be sent around the world without money. But it certainly does occupy more of our time than it probably should.

But this is not about money. It's about looking at a life well lived and seeing what we can learn from it. Kevin lived his life, not to take glory for himself, but to give God all the glory. And Kevin *enjoyed* God. Walking with God daily was not a chore for him. Kevin had to set limits on his morning times with God; otherwise he'd spend all day in prayer and Bible study. One time he told me that spending time with Jesus was his favorite time of the day. God was also glorified in Kevin's death. Tell me that hundreds of people walking and praying seven times around a hospital building doesn't glorify God. And now, what Kevin began as a minimal enjoyment of God on earth is being fully enjoyed by him in heaven for eternity, more than any of us could even imagine. God did answer our prayers to heal Kevin as we walked around the hospital. It was just not in the way we thought it should be.

The Chief End of Man

Glorify God

I've said that the purpose of our lives is to glorify God and enjoy him forever. What does it mean to glorify God? The words *glory* and *glorify* appear repeatedly throughout the Bible. In various places, we are told to live our lives for the *glory of God*, or to *give God glory*, or to *glorify God*. As an example, 1 Corinthians 10:31 says, "So, whether you eat or drink, or whatever you do, do all to the glory of God." This means that everything we do, even the small things, should be done to the glory of God. But what does it mean to do something to the glory of God?

God made us in his image (Genesis 1:27), but most people live in ways that do not reflect his image. That is, they think, feel, and act in ways that do not reflect the image of God. How can we tell if we or others are thinking, feeling, and acting in ways that reflect the image of God? By comparing our lives to Jesus. Paul reminds us in Colossians 1:15 that Jesus is the "image of the invisible God." So, to reflect God's image would be to think, feel, and act in the way and manner of Jesus, following the example he gave us.

Glorifying God is to reflect, or mirror him; to look like him in all that we do. When people look at us, they should see the image of God in our lives. This is what they will see if we are thinking, feeling, and acting like Jesus did. To glorify God means to put God on display in your life as you move about the world. It's to make him look great, displaying all his attributes, in all that we do. We can do this at home, at work, at school, at church, and everywhere else we go. We do this with people and when alone. We do this by how we speak, spend our time, spend our money, and in every choice we make. Every decision will either glorify or not glorify God. If a decision displays the attributes of God, it's glorifying him. If a decision does not display his attributes, it's not glorifying him, and instead likely glorifying us, someone else, or something else.

God is infinitely great, supreme, and perfect beyond comparison, and therefore worthy of glory. He is perfect in love, mercy, justice, faithfulness, holiness, and goodness, and our lives should reflect him in these ways. Glorifying God will result in our praise and adoration, and our obedience to him. We were created for this purpose, to glorify him in all that we are and all that we do.

Finally, God is glorified in tragedy and suffering in at least two ways. First, he is glorified in our tragedy and suffering when we are delivered from it. It may be a miracle or a series of circumstances (mini, hidden miracles) that lead to some deliverance from the tragedy or suffering. Second, he is glorified in our tragedy and suffering when we are *not* delivered from it. This happens when Christians mirror God's image in the face of tragedy and suffering. When tragedy and suffering strike and are horrific, God's people display the attributes of Jesus in their lives. Love, forgiveness, mercy, and peace are attributes that the world knows nothing about and cannot display in the face of tragedy and suffering. When Christians do this, God is glorified.

Enjoy Him Forever

Our purpose in life is to glorify God *and* to enjoy him forever. What does it mean to enjoy God? Enjoying God is to delight in him, prefer him, and be satisfied with him. The best comparison I can think of is the enjoyment of a spouse. I've been married to my wife, Tawny, for over twenty years, and I *enjoy* her. That means, I like being with her, I prefer her over other people, especially over any other woman, and I am satisfied with her. Shouldn't it be this way? As one who has counseled hundreds, maybe thousands, of married individuals, I can say that marriages break when one partner does not enjoy the other, when they stop finding delight in each other, when they prefer other people and things over their spouse.

The Bible compares our relationship with God to a bride with her husband (Isaiah 54:5; Jeremiah 31:32; Revelation 21:2). God delights in us (Psalm 147:11; Zephaniah 3:17), and we should delight in him (Psalm 37:4; Philippians 4:4). What does it look like to enjoy God? How do we know we enjoy God and what should we shoot for if, and when, we don't?

- Enjoying God is looking forward to spending time with him. We do this when we read the Bible, pray, sing, meditate on God and his word, and when we serve or sacrifice for others who are made in God's image.

- Enjoying God is being intellectually stimulated by him, by knowing him and trying to know him deeper.

- Enjoying God is being emotionally stimulated by him, by loving his ways and his commands.

- Enjoying God is wanting our will to line up with his will.

- Enjoying God is preferring him above all other, competing enjoyments.

- Enjoying God forever means that in the ways we enjoy him now, we will for eternity when our life on earth ends. Only then it will be a greater enjoyment.

To glorify God and enjoy him forever is the chief end of humankind, our purpose. But it's often hard to fulfill our purpose. Many of us struggle with this constantly, while some of us go in and out of glorifying God and enjoying him. Why is it so hard? That will be the topic of the next section.

The Competition

Many of us find it hard to live out our purpose: to glorify God and enjoy him forever. As stated above, to glorify God means to mirror the image of Jesus while displaying his attributes in every area of our life, which results in praise, adoration, and obedience. Enjoying God means to prefer him above everyone and everything else so that we really *want* to be with him now and for eternity while humbly submitting to everything he says. For many of us, this is easy on Sunday and hard during the rest of the week. Why is that?

One reason is that there are competing glories and enjoyments. This means just what it sounds like. There are endless people, things, lifestyles, and ideas that compete against God for glory and enjoyment. Anything that puts itself against God as more glorious and more enjoyable, or anything that seems to us more glorious and more enjoyable than God, is one colossal lie. That anything could be worthy of more glory and joy than God is preposterous. Yet how easily we fall into believing it!

One paradigm that stands as a competitor to God for glory and enjoyment is what we call in America, the American dream. Or, as I called it in the last chapter, the Western diet. There is no standard definition for the American dream, so for our discussion, I'll define it this way: *The American dream is the deeply held belief that upward mobility, accomplishments, freedom, and prosperity are the ultimate aim in life, and that these achievements are attainable by everyone and lead to happiness and comfortability, which is desired above all.* There are other ways to define it, but I think you get the idea. It's the idea that we can and should have all that we desire, provided it doesn't hurt anyone else. Health, wealth, prosperity, a nice house, a satisfying job, an enjoyable vacation, a beautiful wife or handsome husband, and happy children. That's what we all want, right? And of course we want God too…let's not forget him.

The American dream is a competing glory and enjoyment, and there are millions of competing glories and enjoyments within the American dream. I wonder if the American-dream lifestyle or paradigm conflicts a bit with the lifestyle and paradigm that God has called us to.

"If anyone comes to me and does not hate his own father and mother and wife and children and brothers and sisters, yes, and even his own life, he cannot be my disciple. Whoever does not bear his own cross and come after me cannot be my disciple… So therefore, any one of you who does not renounce all that he has cannot be my disciple." (Luke 14:26–27, 33)

"Foxes have holes, and birds of the air have nests, but the Son of Man has nowhere to lay his head." (Matthew 8:20)

Indeed, all who desire to live a godly life in Christ Jesus will be persecuted. (2 Timothy 3:12)

I wonder which lifestyle, or paradigm, we choose. I doubt that we can have both. Many try, but there is eventual conflict. I don't think we choose consciously, at least Christians don't. It's hard to imagine a Christian sitting down and saying, "Ok, I know what Jesus says, but I'm going to choose this other thing." The way we could know where our allegiance lies is in how we spend our time and money, what we think most about, and what we most enjoy. The life of many Christians looks more like they are living the American dream than living out discipleship.

The American dream competes for our glory and enjoyment. It's going to be hard to glorify God and enjoy him when there is competition. We can't truly, wholly, and authentically glorify God and enjoy him when we glorify and enjoy something else more. Said another way, we can't live out our purpose for God when we have given something else more importance. And trying to have both never works. Remember, it's a lie that the American dream will give us ultimate happiness, peace, and security. Those things come when we are living out our God-created purpose, to glorify God and enjoy him forever. What stands in the way of living out our purpose? Anything that competes against God for glory and enjoyment; whatever we glory and enjoy more than God.

Destroying the Competition

God loves us too much to let us believe a lie, especially when that lie could cost us our soul. And not only our soul, but our happiness and peace on this earth as well. No one is ever truly happy and peaceful when living in outright rebellion against their Maker, when not living out the purpose for which they were created.

A couple of years ago, we purchased a Nintendo Switch for our boys for Christmas. We were "late to the party," because this was their first gaming console ever, while almost all their friends have had one for most of their lives. Because of the rampant video game addiction I see in kids in my practice, we were very hesitant to let our kids have one. But we reasoned that they are getting older and need to develop self-control around video games. Otherwise, we reasoned, when they move out of our house in a few years, they might fall off the deep end with gaming when they are exposed to the opportunity to play endlessly in their dorm rooms with no one telling them to turn it off.

Our boys were super excited to finally have a gaming system. One of the agreements we made was that if gaming takes priority over school, sports, their relationship with God, or in-person relationships with others, especially with their mom and me, or they develop addictive-type behaviors surrounding gaming (e.g., sneaking gaming when it is not permitted, neglecting responsibilities, having meltdowns when asked to turn off gaming, or not eating or sleeping because of gaming), then gaming is going away. We will not allow an influence in our home that competes with their priorities. We would need to remove, or even destroy, the competition. As a dad who loves his children, I would run the Nintendo Switch over with my car before I would allow it to wreck my children's lives.

Many of us have "Nintendo Switches" in our lives that are in the way of fulfilling our purpose. And because of this, they are in the way of our happiness and peace. Maybe it's the American dream that you've bought in to that has become the priority over glorifying God, and you have given *it* your affections. Whatever it is, God loves you too much to have you miss out on the opportunity to glorify him with your life and enjoy him forever. He may destroy the competition. I don't mean that God will destroy or take away something that is in your way, that he will specifically target the person or thing that has become your priority and that you are giving your affections to. He sometimes will, but that's not usually the case. But it will likely be a tragedy of some type. Something to wake us up from the dream world we've been living in; the one that says we can find happiness and peace elsewhere. Something to get us on track, or back on track, to fulfilling our purpose. God uses tragedy to destroy the competing glories and enjoyments in our lives so that we can fully glorify and enjoy him.

You may have heard the saying, "Don't waste your suffering." When we suffer through tragedy, this is an opportunity to draw closer to God than ever before. Even if your tragedy has led to feelings of anxiety, depression, and anger, God is holding on to you, and he wants you to hold on to him. Experiencing God in tragedy is perhaps the best way to grow deeper in your relationship with him. Depending on God during tragedy is wha will provide the emotional bond that your relationship with him woul lack without it. Without utter dependence on him, your relationship wi God is still in the intellectual phase. Only suffering can produce a lasti emotional connection. Blessings from God do move us to an emotio connection with him, but without suffering, the emotional conne from blessings may only last as long as the blessings do.

Additionally, when we experience tragedy, we should ask, "Are any competing glories and enjoyments that God is trying to destro this tragedy?" Take a good assessment of your life: What do yo about and enjoy, and how do you spend your time and money? D want you to change any of that? Is God trying to cut something ou life? Does God want you to think and feel differently about an change in your life after a tragedy may be exactly what God de complish. And a radical change may be exactly what you need give the tragedy meaning and purpose. Don't let tragedy hap life without being drastically different afterward. Maybe th is a radical lifestyle change, or maybe it's a deeper, more si and relationship with God.

The One Thing Left

I have explained the following four statements in this bo

1. God is in control of all things, including all tragedies, even ones that are due to our sins and the sins of others.

2. All tragedies in this world are within the plan of God, are planned by him, and are either directly or indirectly caused by him or are permitted by him, but even his permission is an indirect causing.

3. All tragedies that we, as Christians, experience are necessary for our good, that is, for our benefit, and they are to result in our repentance, sanctification, or glorification.

Our ultimate purpose in this life and the one after is to glorify ˀod and enjoy him forever, so any tragedy in this life is meant bring us back to or take us deeper in our glorification and ˀment of him.

ˀe all four of the above statements, then there is only one
o do. One thing that still has not been done. One thing
ˀing together and without which we might as well have
journey of trying to understand God in our tragedy
ˀ thing is *surrender*. Surrender. That's it. After all this
ˀll must "do" is to surrender. I put "do" in quotation
ˀng is more like *not* doing something than doing
ˀ. It's not holding your ground or position. It's
ˀender is letting go of your fight against God
ˀ his plan and will for your life as one who
ˀor you because of his great love for you.
ˀke 14 that I didn't mention above when
ˀadigm Jesus calls us to has to do with

unter another king in war,
erate whether he is able
ˀ who comes against him

with twenty thousand? And if not, while the other is yet a great way off, he sends a delegation and asks for terms of peace" (Luke 14:31–32).

Think about this scenario for a moment. If you are a king who realizes that he is doubly outnumbered, what is the most sensible thing to do? Is it to fight? Probably not. The odds are against you: two opposing soldiers against every one of yours. The most sensible thing is to surrender, to ask for terms of peace, in hopes that the opposing king will grant the terms, rather than kill you and every one of your troops.

The picture here is of a humble, sensible, and admittedly weaker king laying down his arms before a more powerful king, saying, "We're not having this fight. You win." I guess this would be nerve-racking in real life against a foreign king, since you don't know whether the king is good or evil. Will he stick to the terms, kill you, or make your life a living hell so that death would have been a better alternative? But if God is the king, if God is the one whom we are laying down our arms for, then we need not worry. He will grant our terms of peace and even more. Jesus' point is in the next verse: "So therefore, any one of you who does not renounce all that he has cannot be my disciple" (Luke 14:33).

The word used here, *renounce*, literally means in Greek to say goodbye (by departing or dismissing). "Say goodbye to all that you have," says Jesus, "*everything.*" In regard to tragedy and suffering, what do we have that we need to say goodbye to? I mean, to what do we need to say goodbye to find happiness and peace in the midst of tragedy and suffering? We already believe the truth about how God is involved in tragedy and suffering, but unless we say goodbye to something, we are going to struggle endlessly in emotional turmoil. That thing is our will. *Our* will. *Our* desires, preferences, motivations, determinations, and wants, if not in line with God's desires, preferences, motivations, determinations, and wants, must be renounced and replaced with his.

One of the most profound mysteries to me is how Jesus was able to say, and really mean, what he prayed in Gethsemane: "Not as I will, but as you will" (Matthew 26:39). Not that he said it, but that he really meant it. I've said or prayed this a million times, but many of those times I don't think I really meant it. Jesus said it and meant it. He knew that he was about to face the worst human suffering and death imaginable. Yet he said, and meant, that while he had a desire to avoid the cross, he had a greater desire to fulfill the cross if that was what God desired. He willed God's will above his own, even though "it was the will of the Lord to crush him" (Isaiah 53:10).

What does this look like in our tragedies and sufferings? My son, who is now fifteen, has been doing Brazilian jiu-jitsu, which is a marital art form of wrestling, for most of his life. I did it with him for a couple of years. Jiu-jitsu emphasizes the use of sparring, which is live training with an opponent to improve your skills and stamina. Holding on to our own will in tragedy and suffering is a lot like wrestling with a stronger, more skilled opponent, which were not hard to find as a white belt. I fought with stronger, more skilled men in every class and got crushed. I was amazed at the technique these guys had. It's like they knew everything I was going to do before I did it and were able to counter with something that would lead to me "tapping out" or surrendering. It was either tap (surrender) or leave with a broken limb. Not surrendering to God's will is like not tapping out. We know there is no way out except to surrender, but instead of surrendering, we end up with a broken limb.

Not surrendering to God in our tragedy is a constant uphill battle that we don't win, and we end up frustrated and *more* hurt. Not surrendering in our tragedy says, and feels, "God, this can't be. You can't do this. This isn't right or fair. I won't let go. I won't accept this. I can't accept this. I will not be ok with what you've done." Surrendering says, and feels, the opposite: "God, this is and can be because you willed it. You *can* do this because you are the Lord of the universe, and my Lord. Everything belongs to you; even I belong to you. Everything you do is right and just. I'm not holding on to this anymore. I accept the worst possible outcome because I know you have my best interest in mind. This world is not my home, and everything works for good in the end."

You know, the crazy thing is, God's will is going to happen anyway. We can choose to accept or resist it. Acceptance leads to peace, while resisting leads to more pain. As we complete this book, let's meditate on the words of Jesus in the Garden of Gethsemane, "Not as I will, but as you will," and pray that we will say it and really mean it in our own lives as we move through the tragedy that the Lord has given.

I hope that our journey together through God's word on the subjects of tragedy and suffering has been fruitful for you. I pray that the thoughts of this book will stay with you and take you deeper into the woods of your cognitive pathway that leads to a better understanding of God's sovereignty over all things, including tragedy and suffering, that this understanding will guard against painful emotions, like anxiety, depression, and anger, and that you will find peace.

Journal Questions

1. Our "chief end" is to glorify God and enjoy him forever. In your own words, describe what this means. How do you feel you are currently doing at glorifying God and enjoying him? Now describe a way that God has been glorified in your tragedy.

2. Describe some of the competing glories and enjoyments that are blocking you from glorifying and enjoying God more fully.

3. Think about a tragedy that you have gone through or are currently going through. Is God trying to do something in your life through this tragedy? If so, what? Are there competing glories and enjoyments he is trying to destroy? If so, what are they?

4. In what ways, if any, have you changed since experiencing your tragedy?

5. In tragedy and suffering, we must surrender our will to God's will. What does this mean for you in your tragedy? How do you feel you are doing at surrendering to God's will? What can you do today to surrender to God's will in your tragedy?

Conclusion

Tragedy is inevitable. Devasting emotions are optional. How we *think* about tragedy will affect how we *feel* when tragedy comes. If we believe that forces other than God are finally, or ultimately, responsible for ou tragic situation, then we will more likely experience anxiety, depression, anger during and following tragedy. A belief that God is final, or ultima in all tragic situations, is the path toward finding peace in tragedy. Thi ing about the all-encompassing love of God, who loved us so much he died for us, produces peace when we realize that God is also sove over every tragedy. The God who loves us is also sovereign. God is all-loving and all-powerful. No tragedy is bigger than him. Any dist emotion can be put in check as we consider these facts.

I have presented a biblical case for God's rule over various tragedy: death, disease, disaster, and even despicable evil. That dains all things that come to pass is both biblical, and the only r conclusion when considering the other options, for example, does *not* ordain all things, and that some things are left out o and in the hand of another force, or chance. That is not the the Bible presents, and not one that we can defend or believe encompassing view of God's sovereignty is the only one tha peace in the face of tragedy.

Not only should we understand God's rulership over all ing tragedy, but we should understand that suffering wa plan from the very beginning. Additionally, all our sufferi in his book before any of them came to be. It was all pl story that you and I are living right now. In many ways our lives are like a story. There is a protagonist, or main character, in the story. This is us, you and I. You are the focus of your own personal story. In this story, you'll meet several tertiary characters. These are people in your life who are supportive, some more, some less. Not necessarily in your inner circle, but around you. Then there are deuteragonists. These are the people who are in your inner circle. Let's say a spouse, family, and close friends. And of course, no story would be complete without an antagonist. Maybe several. These are the people who come into your life that are unsupportive and v harm or try to harm you.

n any story, unless you read the spoiler, you don't know the ending. n't even know what is going to happen on the next page. You must ding. This is partly true in real life. We don't know what's going tomorrow. A night in a dungeon could end with a morning in 'e don't know what circumstance time will bring. We've seen s happened, even to God's people, throughout the Bible. And 'ives, faithful Christians receiving persecution, getting can-bling accidents, and dying young. We are not promised a nor can we know what tragedies will happen to us. Jesus we will have tribulation (John 16:33). But when and tion? We don't know; we must *keep reading*.

s are like a story in that we don't know what's going t this is only partly true. It's partly true because, paragraph, we don't know the details or specific ing. But we do know many things. Yes, even ils and circumstances. Not the details and t what happens *in* them. For example, in ve us peace (John 16:33), and in affliction hians 1:4). Even in suffering, God will 4:19) and will give us peace when we t know what we will experience, but

n (Psalm 121) and blessing (Psalm tood, in the face of unspeakable raul realize or understand God's protection and blessing as he sat in a prison cell awaiting his execution? Or how could John the Baptist, who was eventually beheaded, realize and understand God's protection and blessing as he was unjustly thrown into Herod's prison? Well, it must be understood differently than anyone in the world would understand protection and blessing. The non-Christian world sees protection as *not* being thrown into prison or beheaded. It sees blessing as a life of success, prosperity, and physical comfort. Certainly not things that the Apostle Paul or John the Baptist had, but protection and blessing they had, nonetheless. It takes a spiritual lens to see God's protection and blessing during tragedy, and we should look for these promises when we experience a tragedy.

The Outcome of Our Tragedy

I think most importantly, we know a good deal about the outcome of our tragedy. As I said, we may not have details, but we do have the overall conclusion. Like reading the spoiler for a movie, you know the basic conclusion, but not every little detail. The outcome of every tragedy that a Christian will ever experience is found in Romans 8:28. This well-known scripture speaks to God's people throughout the ages: "And we know that for those who love God all things work together for good, for those who are called according to his purpose." *All things.* Not that all things are good, but that God works all things together *for* good. The tragedies discussed in this book are not good. Death, disease, disaster, and despicable evil are heartbreaking tragedies that are not good. But God works so that events like death, disease, disaster, and despicable evil turn out for good, for *our* good. And he is always working (John 5:17).

It is amazing to think about how God does this. Think of the billions of details that need to occur for specific good to be worked into every tragic situation Christians experience. Sometimes we can clearly see the good God is working, and sometimes we cannot. It is often the fight of our faith to look for good in every tragic situation. In every tragedy, we can know that good is either here, or coming, even if we can't see it. This is where faith comes in. We walk by faith, not by sight (2 Corinthians 5:7). This is important to remember when experiencing tragedy.

It's helpful to journal when you have experienced a tragedy. Not only journaling your thoughts and feelings and answering the journal questions in this book, but specifically writing out all the good things that you can find that have come from the tragedy. This will be hard at first. But forcing yourself to think of, find, and write every good thing that has come from the tragedy is important to help shape how you are thinking and feeling.

You may be thinking, as I have often thought, *"It's impossible to find any good in my tragedy."* If that is true, and you are a person who loves God, then Romans 8:28 is either untrue or God has just not worked good into it *yet*. Remember, Romans 8:28 is a promise, but it is not a promise with a decided timeline. So don't throw the promise out the window. When you throw out one promise, what's stopping you from dismissing others? These are dangerous waters. I have known people of great faith who have completely abandoned the faith during times of tragedy. In their minds, they just can't continue to follow a God who would allow such a thing to happen. They have in their mind the wrong God. Or in the language we have used in this book, their cognitive pathway stops short.

Fighting the good fight of the faith (1 Timothy 6:12) is a good way to describe the Christian experience during tragedy. It really is a fight to see the good in a tragic situation. But fight we must. Satan desires that your tragic situation would destroy your faith, while God desires it for your good (e.g., Genesis 50:20). Sometimes your good is visible and material, while at other times it's purely spiritual, such as a change of heart. Pain does bring gain. But it can instead bring bitterness if we are not careful.

I've been talking about people who love God and experience a tragedy. But what about people who don't love God? What happens when they experience a tragedy? I won't go into many details here but will just mention one person in the Bible who stands out as an example: King Nebuchadnezzar. King Nebuchadnezzar was the arrogant pagan king of the Babylonian Empire who gazed upon the great city from the roof of his palace and said, "Is not this great Babylon, which I have built by my mighty power as a royal residence and for the glory of my majesty?" (Daniel 4:30). Immediately following this haughty statement, Nebuchadnezzar's sanity was taken from him, and he "was driven from among men and ate grass like an ox, and his body was wet with the dew of heaven till his hair grew as long as eagles' feathers, and his nails were like birds' claws" (Daniel 4:33).

This was a serious judgment. King Nebuchadnezzar's tragedy was predicted by the prophet Daniel, from Nebuchadnezzar's own dream twelve months prior (Daniel 4:19–27). Daniel even warned Nebuchadnezzar to repent, stating that repentance might bring a "lengthening" of Nebuchadnezzar's prosperity (Daniel 4:27). Proverbs 16:18 says, "Pride goes before destruction, and a haughty spirit before a fall." This judgment upon King Nebuchadnezzar was not wholly destructive, but *restorative*. God's intention was to humble this proud king; to change his heart and how he thought. Seven whole years were needed to bring about this change. At the end of that time, when Nebuchadnezzar's reason returned to him, he said, "Now I, Nebuchadnezzar, praise and extol and honor the King of heaven, for all his works are right and his ways are just; and those who walk in pride he is able to humble" (Daniel 4:37).

King Nebuchadnezzar did not love, honor, or listen to God. He was a self-reliant, self-focused, and egotistical man. But God did not let him stay that way. How was a man like this, with unfathomable worldly power, wealth, and success going to change? *Suffering.* Often that is the only thing that will get our attention. As C. S. Lewis observed, "The human spirit will not even begin to try to surrender self-will as long as all seems to be well with it... But pain insists upon being attended to. God whispers to us in our pleasures, speaks in our conscience, but shouts in our pain: it is His megaphone to rouse a deaf world."[47] Our tragedy is God's megaphone. He is shouting for change. For Christians and non-Christians, tragedy is meant to take us deeper in our reliance upon him and our love for him.

The Ultimate Outcome of Our Story

I explained that we know a good deal about the outcome of our tragedy. But we also know the ultimate outcome of our story. The outcome of our tragedy is that God is working in it to bring about good, often a spiritual good, like a change of mind and heart. But what is the ultimate outcome of our story? I mean, how does our story end? I am presently writing this "Conclusion" chapter in an airport in Venice, Italy. My wife and I just finished a two-week trip through Italy, and part of our trip included a tour of Rome. In Rome, we visited the Colosseum and Nero's Circus, which is presently located in Vatican City. These two locations originally welcomed thousands of Roman spectators who came to watch Christians die in the arena less than two thousand years ago. It was said that the Apostles Peter and Paul were executed in Nero's Circus.

What was the ultimate outcome of their story and that of countless other martyrs who have died over the centuries? Some of them died so suddenly that there was no time for a spiritual change of mind and heart. Or how about the faithful Christian men and women who did not die as martyrs, but maybe in their beds after a long, successful, and comfortable life? Or disciples of Jesus who died young, in horrible pain, and who never experienced success or comfort? Or babies and children who die? We know the ultimate outcome of their story, and our story, and can take comfort in it. The Apostle Paul, in 1 Corinthians 4:16–18, said:

> So we do not lose heart. Though our outer self is wasting away, our inner self is being renewed day by day. For this light momentary affliction is preparing for us an eternal weight of glory beyond all comparison, as we look not to the things that are seen but to the things that are unseen. For the things that are seen are transient, but the things that are unseen are eternal.

The ultimate outcome of our story is an "eternal weight of glory beyond all comparison." What is this eternal weight of glory? To answer this question, we need to understand the context in which Paul is writing to the church in Corinth. In this same chapter, Paul describes being "afflicted in every way, but not crushed; perplexed, but not driven to despair; persecuted, but not forsaken; struck down, but not destroyed;" (2 Corinthians 4:8–9). *Afflicted, perplexed, persecuted*, and *struck down*. These are all devasting blows that happened to the Corinthian Christians. But in all this, they were not *crushed, driven to despair, forsaken*, or *destroyed*. Why? Because these blows were preparing them for something. They were preparing them for an eternal weight of glory.

The afflictions, persecutions, and situations that caused them to be perplexed and struck down were the things that were getting them ready for something that was beyond all comparison. Better, and more amazing, by comparison, to anything they could have experienced in their life, or ever asked for or thought (Ephesians 3:20). In comparison to eternity, which is presently unseen, everything that is presently seen is momentary. In comparison to the weight of glory, which is also presently unseen, all amount of affliction, which is presently seen, is light. Affliction is seen but light and momentary; glory is unseen but weighty and eternal.

This is what is waiting for us. This is the ultimate outcome of our story: an eternal weight of glory beyond all comparison. The eternal weight of glory beyond all comparison is God the Father; and it is him gifting us with eternal life in Christ Jesus his Son in heaven after all suffering has passed away. That is the ultimate outcome of our story. That's how the story ends. It ends with a glory that is weighty and eternal. How and when will we get there? None of us knows. That is the end for sure, but how and when is different for everyone.

Everyone will have their own path. Some paths will be marked by pain, suffering, and tragedy. Death, disease, disaster, and despicable evils will pave the way, preparing us for an eternal weight of glory. But Paul said that it is affliction that prepares us for the eternal weight of glory. How do afflictions prepare us? Present afflictions prepare us to accept, embrace, love, and appreciate the gracious gift of salvation that is coming to us by our heavenly Father. Yes, every affliction, great or small, is preparing us for the eternal weight of glory. Every pain, every loss, every tragedy, every moment of affliction and suffering is getting us ready to receive the eternal weight of glory that is beyond all comparison.

How should we think about every affliction that befalls us? It's all preparation for something amazing. And not just amazing, but *weighty*. Too weighty to lift in our current condition. Think about affliction as making us stronger so that we can carry the heavy weight of eternal glory once it is given to us. And the more affliction we receive in this life, the stronger we will be, and the better able we'll be to carry the eternal weight of glory that is beyond comparison.

13. Piper, J. (2008). *Spectacular Sins*. Crossway.

14. Piper, J. (2013). *Five Points: Towards a Deeper Experience of God's Grace*. Christian Focus.

15. Piper, J. (2021). *Providence*. Crossway.

16. Pink, A. W. (2008). *The Sovereignty of God*. Wilder.

17. Sproul, R. C. (1994). *Surprised by Suffering*. Tyndale House Publishers.

18. Sproul, R. C. (2017). *What Is Reformed Theology?* Ligonier Ministries.

19. Spurgeon, C. H. (2011). *Spurgeon's Sermons*. Hendrickson Pub.

20. Tada, J. E. (2010). *A Place of Healing: Wrestling with the Mysteries of Suffering, Pain, and God's Sovereignty*. David C Cook.

URGENT PLEA!

Thank You for Reading My Book!
I really appreciate all your feedback,
and I love hearing what you have to say.
I need your input to make the next version
of this book and my future books better.

Please take two minutes now to leave a helpful review on
Amazon letting me know what you thought of the book:
Thanks so much!
– *Dr. Messina*

About the Author

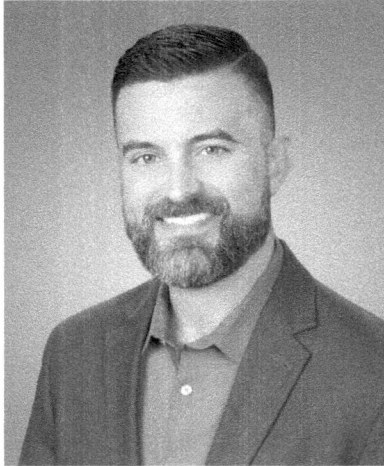

Dr. Michael Messina, a licensed clinical psychologist and Christian counselor, is the founder of Dr. Messina & Associates, a mental health private practice in Texas. With two decades of experience in psychotherapy, psychological testing, and Christian counseling, he specializes in treating anxiety, depression, and trauma. A former pastor, he has held academic positions and frequently lectures at various institutions. Dr. Messina has also collaborated with media outlets such as CBS and CNBC. Passionate about integrating his Christian faith into clinical practice, Dr. Messina's work is a beacon of hope for those grappling with tragedy. He has been married for 21 years and has two sons.

References

Introduction
1. Association, A. P. (2022). *Diagnostic and Statistical Manual of Mental Disorders: DSM-5-TR.*
2. Lewis, C. S. (2002). *The Problem of Pain.* HarperCollins.
3. Keller, T. (2015). *Walking with God Through Pain and Suffering.* Penguin Books.

Chapter 1: Think Differently
4. Beck, A. T. (1979). *Cognitive Therapy of Depression.* Guilford Press.
5. Piper, J. (2008). *Spectacular Sins.* Crossway.

Chapter 2: Cognitive Pathways
6. The American Institute of Stress. (n.d.). Holmes-Rahe stress inventory. Retrieved July 6, 2024, from https://www.stress.org/holmes-rahe-stress-inventory

Chapter 3: Going Deeper
7. Piper, J. (2021). *Providence.* Crossway.

Chapter 4: Anxiety
8. Anxiety and Depression Association of America. (n.d.). Facts & statistics. Retrieved July 6, 2024, from https://adaa.org/understanding-anxiety/facts-statistics
9. Association, A. P. (2022). *Diagnostic and Statistical Manual of Mental Disorders: DSM-5-TR.*
10. McEwen, B. S. (2010). Stress, sex, and neural adaptation to a changing environment: Mechanisms of neuronal remodeling. *Physiology & Behavior, 99*(2), 151–157. https://www.ncbi.nlm.nih.gov/pmc/articles/PMC2940247/
11. Holland, K. & Legg, T. J. (2022, June 9). Effects of anxiety on the body. *Healthline.* https://www.healthline.com/health/anxiety/effects-on-body#how-does-it-feel

Chapter 5: Depression
12. Centers for Disease Control and Prevention. (2022, April 8). Mental health and genetics. https://www.cdc.gov/genomics/resources/diseases/mental.htm
13. Depression and Bipolar Support Alliance. (n.d.). Depression statistics. Retrieved July 6, 2024, from https://www.dbsalliance.org/education/depression/statistics/
14. Association, A. P. (2022). *Diagnostic and Statistical Manual of Mental Disorders: DSM-5-TR.*

Conclusion
47. Lewis, C. S. (2002). *The Problem of Pain*. HarperCollins.

Milton Keynes UK
Ingram Content Group UK Ltd.
UKHW021842301124
451618UK00019BA/419/J